SAVING CHIMPANZEES

SAVING CHIMPANZEES

A MAN ON A RESCUE MISSION

Eugene Cussons

PENGUIN BOOKS

PENGUIN BOOKS

Published by the Penguin Group
Penguin Books (South Africa) (Pty) Ltd, 24 Sturdee Avenue, Rosebank,
Johannesburg 2196, South Africa
Penguin Group (USA) Inc, 375 Hudson Street, New York, New York 10014,
USA
Penguin Group (Canada), 90 Eglinton Avenue East, Suite 700, Toronto,
Ontario, Canada M4P 2Y3 (a division of Pearson Penguin Canada Inc)
Penguin Books Ltd, 80 Strand, London WC2R 0RL, England
Penguin Ireland, 25 St Stephen's Green, Dublin 2, Ireland (a division of
Penguin Books Ltd)
Penguin Group (Australia), 250 Camberwell Road, Camberwell, Victoria 3124,
Australia (a division of Pearson Australia Group Pty Ltd)
Penguin Books India Pvt Ltd, 11 Community Centre, Panchsheel Park, New
Delhi – 110 017, India
Penguin Group (NZ), 67 Apollo Drive, Mairangi Bay, Auckland 1310, New
Zealand (a division of Pearson New Zealand Ltd)

Penguin Books (South Africa) (Pty) Ltd, Registered Offices:
24 Sturdee Avenue, Rosebank, Johannesburg 2196, South Africa

www.penguinbooks.co.za

First published by Penguin Books (South Africa) (Pty) Ltd 2011
Reprinted 2011

ISBN 978-0-14-352813-5

Typeset by Nix Design in Bell MT
Cover by mrdesign
Cover photograph courtesy of Animal Planet
Printed and bound by Interpak Books, Pietermartizburg

For my wife Natasha
and
my daughter Haley

Author's Note

Some names have been changed to protect
the identities of the individuals concerned.

CONTENTS

PROLOGUE
SUDAN

A slight breeze rustles the branches of the acacia thorn tree and provides a little welcome relief for all who are sheltering under it, trying to escape the unrelenting sun.

I am resting on top of a plastic sky kennel travel crate containing two of the chimpanzees that we travelled here to rescue and relocate to the Chimp Eden sanctuary on my family's game reserve in South Africa.

The saturated red clay soil makes it difficult and unpleasant to pace up and down, something I would otherwise be doing right now. It's been four weeks since I arrived on this dirt strip in Rumbek, Sudan.

Delay after delay postponed the return leg of the rescue mission to the sanctuary. Nothing on this mission had so far gone according to plan and I had hoped desperately that today would be different.

Sue Knight, the owner of the 'safe house' where the five chimpanzees had been cared for until a flight out could be arranged, puffs nervously on a cigarette while her eyes remain fixed on the red earth beneath her feet. Living out here in the small outpost of Rumbek cannot be easy for Sue and her husband who manages a small aircraft refuelling depot. Both of us are eager to see the Hercules C-130 cargo aircraft that should touch down any minute now, or at least we are hoping it will. With so much already having gone wrong, I am actually beginning to expect the worst.

Both of us opted to wait for the aircraft at the end of the airfield, which we approached via a small access road. Strictly speaking, we are not allowed to be waiting here but the risk of being cornered by an official outweighs drawing unnecessary attention to ourselves at the small Customs building at the other end of the airfield. Many Sudanese seem to gather at the decrepit building; it almost seems to hold the same attraction for them as a watering hole has for animals during the dry season. Being white makes us an automatic target for money extortion by corrupt police and government officials who would like nothing better than giving us the alternative of rotting away in jail.

Out of nowhere a dilapidated green Land Cruiser pickup truck appears and races past us, screeching to a halt less than fifty yards away. A ragtag bunch of soldiers disembark unceremoniously. One of them barks orders and motions wildly with one hand while clutching his AK-47 in the other. The rest scatter off to several places along the mile-long runway and assume what look to be securing positions.

From experience I know that the presence of soldiers in this country is bad news and at this point we are totally compromised. Not only are we not supposed to be here, but we are also encumbered with three crates of chimpanzees. I get off the crate I have been sitting on and try as unobtrusively as possible to move in behind one of the small crates. I bend down, keeping my face averted so that I can avoid eye contact with any of the soldiers staring our way.

Sue murmurs something like 'Shit!' and blanches. She turns her back on the soldiers and stares at me as if I might come up with some bright idea. A few tense minutes pass and I realise that the plane is suspiciously late. It was supposed to have landed at ten-thirty, but the presence of the soldiers hints at the possibility that the airfield might have been closed to accommodate the arrival of a high-ranking official or, worse, a military commander. I snatch the satellite phone out of my side pocket and punch the redial button. A few seconds pass and then a male voice answers: 'Safair Marketing. Good day.' I immediately reply, 'Darian, it's Eugene Cussons. I hope you fellows have not forsaken us here in the sticks.'

He hardly gives me time to finish my sentence. 'Eugene! Thank goodness you've phoned. I've been trying without luck to get hold of you.' He doesn't have to say much more than that because I'm already expecting the worst. I know that his next words will spell disaster but I am still willing to hear them. Time seems to slow down but my heart rate rockets in anticipation of bad news and a giant knot forms in my throat, followed by a cold sweat that breaks out on my forehead.

'We can't land in Rumbek,' he says. 'The tower in El Obeid radioed the aircraft refusing it permission to land. They have warned us that there will be severe consequences should we try to do so. I don't know what to say. The flight plan was approved weeks ago but for some inexplicable reason they are now denying us permission to land when the aircraft was already on its way. It's been told to continue to the refuelling location at Entebbe in Uganda.'

For a second or two I can't get myself to answer him. My mind is racing, trying to think of a solution, to plead with him to find a way to make it happen. I look up briefly at the soldiers, turn my back on them and start to walk away. I cup my hand over the phone microphone in order to muffle my loud response.

'What the hell do you mean, you can't land? What am I supposed to do now?'

Darian's answer is predictable. 'I don't know …' An uncomfortable silence follows as he waits for my reaction.

'Give me some time to think, Darian. I'll phone you back. Just stay close to the phone!'

As I stand up to face the menacing soldiers my overactive imagination conjures up the headline: *Eugene Cussons apprehended in southern Sudan – stranded with five chimpanzees on a dirt strip in the middle of nowhere with only three dollars in his pocket.*

Involuntarily, I wipe the fresh outbreak of sweat off my face, my wet shirt already clinging to my body in the sweltering heat. The damn aircraft that was supposed to take us all to safety has not pitched up. It's a hopeless situation … I must think fast, find a way out of this mess. If I can only avoid trouble … the last thing I want to do is have to return the chimps to the temporary 'safe house' and tie them to the very same trees I had sworn to rescue them from. Now some distance away, I notice the soldiers staring at me.

I'm a guy who always makes a plan, but not this time. I reproach myself: 'How the hell did I land us in such a mess?' I curse uselessly under my breath and run both my hands through my hair in despair as I mouth quietly, 'Think, think, dammit … think!'

Feigning a nonchalance I certainly do not feel, I furiously run through the possibilities. I know full well there is no other lifeline here. I will have to come up with a solution myself, and fast, as the only plane that can get us back to South Africa is probably already making its way from El Obeid to Entebbe. Their intended landing in strife-torn south Sudan must have set off alarm bells somewhere.

At that very moment Nina starts to make warning calls from the inside of her crate. '*Uwhoo, uwhoo ...*' Her calls are promptly answered by some of the other chimps until the combined vocalisations become impossibly loud and start to draw the attention of the wrong people. Most of the soldiers turn to stare at the crates. Sue bends down and tries to pacify the chimps but to no avail.

The rescue mission is on the brink of failure. I murmur to myself, 'We're screwed!'

ONE

THE BEGINNING

The youngest child of three, I grew up in the north-eastern Low-veld region of South Africa where I was born in 1979. With an older brother and sister, my early life was anything but uneventful. We lived on a game reserve, which instilled in me a great love of nature, and some irresponsible behaviour besides. One of my first memories is of my brother and me entering buildings abandoned by humans but inhabited by swarms of bees for the sole reason of seeing who could fight his way out with the least damage.

I did not, at that stage, hear the call to save the great apes from extinction, but one thing I learned early on was that the conservation of animals is the key to the preservation of humans. When I was a child my father, who was a civil engineer by trade, used his other skill as a helicopter pilot to assist in game capture operations on game farms and ranches in the old Transvaal province. The captured animals were sold to game farmers, and the excess or unwanted ones were relocated to my home at Umhloti Nature Reserve in Mpumalanga where they were given a new lease on life and where my father insisted that no sport hunting should be allowed.

I was exposed to the ways of managing a nature reserve from a young age and I was taught that managing life often means that you have to take it; sometimes one has to track sick or injured animals that would have to be put out of their misery, or removed, to ensure the safety of both humans and other animals. So I learned the necessary tracking and hunting skills that enabled me to assist in such efforts from time to time.

But these weren't my only skills. I have always had a great thirst for adventure, mastering every adventurous skill I came across – rock climbing, sky diving, piloting, scuba diving, free diving, even my explorers rating as an off-road driving instructor.

It was, however, during my high school days that I learned real survival skills; navigating teenage challenges and schoolyard bullies proved daunting at times. When I moved to a new high school for my final two years I found myself in a new and different environment, one that offered me an opportunity for personal growth and development, an opportunity to become any kind of person I wanted to be, to embark on a sort of personal social experiment, if you like. This was the part of my life that I'm most proud of, finding the courage to swim upstream and becoming someone who would not be afraid of anything life threw at him.

So I began to reinvent myself, changing from an introvert into the complete opposite. It was a journey of self-discovery and transformation, and it worked. I learned how to set myself a goal and how to chase it down by whatever means were needed.

All good things come to an end, they say, and so did my teenage years. I had to decide what to do with my life, and it included further education. However, I wasn't completely done with my personal social experiment and instead of further study in the field of conservation, I decided to study economics. This was probably the best thing I could have done, for not only did I enjoy the 'bigger picture' but it gave me the skills to identify opportunities and to make them work. There was just one small problem: I'm not really fond of money. To elaborate on that, it's not *having* money that I hate, but what money does to people and to those closest to them. Nevertheless, by the end of my second year at university I had set up my own IT company. Some of my educators found my venture so appealing that they joined me, and eventually I found myself in the situation of working with my professors in a business venture only to sit in their classrooms later in the day.

As someone who is passionate about conservation and who loves animals more than almost anything else, I had played out my life experiment to the point where I was forced to make the most important decision of my life. I had started a company that was all about making money – something that in itself I found uninspiring. I received an attractive offer to purchase the company and wondered whether I should sell it. But somewhere along the line it became clear that I'd be selling out my partners if I did this, which made me somewhat despondent. I was not convinced that this was the sort of life I wanted, and I have to admit that the prospect of never again living in the bush had been bothering me for some time.

One night while contemplating my predicament I had a discussion with my father on the phone and he said exactly what I needed to hear: leave what makes you unhappy and do what makes you feel alive. I closed down my company, packed my bags and headed back home to develop a game lodge on Umhloti Nature Reserve.

This was round about 2004 and I still had not heard the call to save the great apes from extinction. And it was another year before I crossed paths with a volunteer from the Jane Goodall Institute (JGI). Peta told me how the JGI had been struggling to create a chimpanzee sanctuary in South Africa and outlined the reasons why it was so necessary for there to be a sanctuary in this country. There were many chimpanzees in Africa that had been orphaned as a result of the bush meat trade, or displaced from their habitat because of war and instability throughout much of their range. There was no possibility of setting up sanctuaries for these chimps in the countries concerned. For one thing, it was simply too expensive and, for another, there was the ever present risk of new conflicts breaking out. South Africa, as one of the few stable countries on the continent, could offer a safe haven for chimpanzees and the costs of caring for them would be relatively cheap compared with other African countries. Peta also told me that at the turn of the twentieth century there had been about two million chimpanzees still in the wild and that now there were fewer than 200 000.

This time I heard the call, and the very next week I contacted JGI's executive director in South Africa to offer the Umhloti Nature Reserve as a possible venue for the establishment of a sanctuary for chimpanzees.

I will never forget the expression on my father's face the first time I put the idea to him. 'Chimps in the Lowveld?' he said. 'Are you mad?' It took some persuading, but eventually he and my brother came round to the idea. I convinced my family that they should join me in a venture to build a sanctuary of the highest quality.

When we finally reached an agreement with the JGI, the application process to the Parks Authority would be put in motion.

Then came the business side of things. The first hurdle proved one of the most difficult because the JGI was not really set up in South Africa to deal with chimpanzee conservation. Up to the time of our proposal the JGI had already attempted to develop a sanctuary on four different occasions, but had not been successful in doing so. There was a variety of reasons why these attempts failed, but it was mostly due to lack of funding and negative results from environmental impact assessments. Also, they did not actually have the expertise in South Africa to work with chimpanzees, or even the expertise to assist in designing a sanctuary.

After detailed consultation with the Parks Authority, it became clear that the only way a chimpanzee sanctuary could be established in South Africa was if it was a self-sustaining organisation, which meant it would need to rely, to a large extent, on tourism. And since we were proposing to build the sanctuary on our game reserve, we as a family would be personally liable for any illegal conduct that might take place there.

It was by no means an easy venture, but one thing that comforted me was that apparently there would be no difficulty identifying orphan chimpanzees. During early discussions a foreign consultant to JGI South Africa informed me that there were chimpanzee orphans all over Africa and that locating them and planning their rescue was not worth further investigation and planning at that early stage of the process. Being inexperienced in these matters, I accepted this statement at face value and didn't give it another thought. In the event, however, we were to find that our assumption that we would have the cooperation of the countries concerned, as well as the international community, proved wrong.

It took more than a year to finalise the signing of an agreement with JGI South Africa. It was now up to me to begin the application process with the Parks Authority, which was known to be a difficult one; it had in fact proved an insurmountable obstacle for previous attempts by the JGI.

If I had known just how difficult and lengthy the process would be I would probably have keeled over and abandoned the effort right then and there. The procedure involved our having to employ experts, build facilities and commission environmental impact assessments, all without any clear assurance that the project would get an operating licence, despite the Parks Authority's earlier intimation that the model we had proposed would be accepted. It was a huge leap of faith and an enormous financial risk on the part of my family.

However, the call to help the great apes was strong and this invisible driving force kept me going and kept me motivating and convincing everyone that it was the right thing to do. Yet I myself was completely inexperienced and every step of the way became a journey of discovery for me.

But it wasn't all gloom and doom. I had been researching chimpanzees thoroughly and had found two great ape specialists to design the facilities. I involved myself with the design process so that I could understand the reasoning that went into it. I did not even have one day's experience of working with chimps and there is a big difference between learning on paper how to work with them and actually being in the same room with them.

But this was about to change. We had an unexpected phone call from the head of the ministry of forestry in Angola. He had heard by chance that we were building a chimpanzee sanctuary and contacted me in the belief that we would be able to assist in solving his country's great ape orphan problems. What should have been a visit by the JGI's chairman turned into a trip to Angola by myself and Eric du Bois, who was my Swiss primate expert at the time.

This would be my introduction to what the JGI was all about. Luckily for me, we were going to be staying with an expatriate South African family who had an infant chimpanzee running rampant in their home. So I would have my first contact with a chimp! This was an exciting thought, but it also underlined to me the serious nature of the project we had embarked on. We were building a captive facility for animals that are known to be violent and dangerous. This was not something to be taken lightly, but our commitment to the cause of the great apes was strong and we knew, scary though it might have been, that we were doing the right thing.

The young chimp was anything but a killer; she had a great personality and was extremely playful. In many ways she was like a human child with attention deficit disorder who was being treated with regular doses of Redbull! Sally was her name and she had had three different families taking care of her. All the families worked for the massive Grinaker-LTA company and they lived in their employer's staff compound, which contained more than fifty houses neatly organised into streets and somewhat reminiscent of an American suburban neighbourhood. Sally was adorable but alien to me, so I kept my distance and watched the experienced Eric interact with her.

We were taken on a tour of Luanda by Dr Almeida from the ministry of forestry, visiting all the sites where the chimpanzee orphans were being held. It was to be a life-changing experience for me.

The first site we visited was a hardware store near the centre of the city. We travelled along rundown roads bustling with vehicles and people, each clearly more eager to arrive at their destination than the next. With no traffic lights and bumper-to-bumper vehicles, the mere eight-mile journey took us more than three hours and left me with a splitting headache.

Finally, we arrived at the Maquil hardware store. It was unlike anything I had ever seen before with its entrance barricaded with a giant steel door that must have been at least ten feet high. Dr Almeida knocked on a smaller access door alongside and was promptly answered. In medieval fashion, a small slit in the door at eye level slid open to reveal the eyes of the doorman. Dr Almeida flashed his government identity card and we were let into a courtyard where a few men were gathered around a makeshift cage with black steel bars. It was about six feet high and the same in width and the interior was completely dark, offering no clue to the identity of its occupant.

The men were evidently amused by something, laughing and gesturing at the seemingly empty cage. Imagine my surprise when a thin hairy arm reached through the bars from the dark interior. The tiny cage was home to what looked like an emaciated adult chimpanzee. In utter disbelief I moved closer but the man nearest the cage abruptly halted my approach. 'You must watch out!' he barked in broken English.

But by this time I was close enough to get a good look at the female chimp. Inquisitively, she pressed her face up against the bars, obviously interested in the new faces. She stared at us for a moment and then did something strange. In a single rehearsed motion she shook her head up and down and from side to side and then walked from one side of the structure to the other. Fixing her gaze on me and Eric, she extended her arm as far as she could towards us. It seemed to me as though she wanted to make contact but, having already been warned, I wasn't going to move any closer.

She was in an extremely emaciated condition. I didn't have to be a primatologist to realise that this chimpanzee was terribly unhappy. When I refused her invitation for contact she retracted her arm and continued her head-shaking routine, pacing up and down the front of the cage. I looked into her eyes and felt overwhelmed with sadness. She wanted out … surely I wasn't the only person who could see this?

Just then the owner, a Mr Jose da Silva, arrived. He was about seventy years old, a short frail man with grey hair. 'Bon dia!' he greeted us warmly. He continued to utter a few phrases before he realised that we did not speak Portuguese. He then directed his attention towards Dr Almeida who nodded in agreement at everything he said. Mr da Silva ushered everyone into his office but it turned out that we were a chair short, so I excused myself from the sit-down and left Eric to deal with things.

I was drawn to the female chimpanzee who was still restlessly pacing up and down the cage. I found it difficult to believe that anyone could keep a chimpanzee in such a confined space – and with no direct sunlight. I walked towards the man who was still standing in front of the cage, but this time I edged closer, intent on seeing whether the chimpanzee would again extend her arm and try to touch me. I calculated what I perceived to be a safe distance from her reach and bravely stood firm.

The man warned me again: 'Careful, Lika grab you …' he had hardly finished speaking when she flung her arm out towards me and to my horror I realised that I had completely misjudged her reach. She grabbed at my shirt pocket and had actually got most of her hand inside before I could react. Fortunately, there was nothing in the pocket. She pulled back her hand and held her fingers to her nose, smelling them.

My surprised but belated response was to stumble backwards over some piping, coming to rest on my behind, much to the amusement of the man who offered me a hand to help me to my feet. I gathered myself together immediately and tried a different approach. I extended my hand towards her to see what her response would be. Her behaviour was once again surprising. Instead of lunging at me, she reached out calmly and took hold of my hand. Maintaining her light grip on my hand, she slowly pulled me closer.

At this point the man felt compelled to warn me again, but I interrupted him. 'It's okay, it's okay,' I said softly. She tried to pull my hand into the cage. I balled my hand into a fist to make sure she couldn't take a bite at my fingers, and placed my arm horizontally against the bars to prevent her from pulling it into the cage..

Her attitude changed from calm to excited as she fixed her eyes on my arm. She started to roll her tongue in her mouth and excitedly began to pick at my skin, stroking the hair on my arm as if searching for something that didn't belong. I didn't sense any threatening behaviour from her – just a chimp who looked like she wanted to be friends. I moved my gaze to her eyes. As if sensing this, she looked up at me. It was a moment I won't forget as long as I live. Eric had told me that the same kind of experience was what drew him to dedicate his life to chimpanzees. The first time you look into the eyes of a chimpanzee you know that they are different, that there is some sort of consciousness there that is different from that of any other animal.

Lika was thirteen years old. She had spent her days in that tiny prison and she had developed some erratic behaviour because of it. But there *was* something I could do about it. Even if I didn't meet another chimp on that trip, the encounter with sweet, desperate Lika was enough for me to understand what the cause was all about. It was all that was needed to convince me that, no matter what it took, I would get every single chimpanzee orphan I could find back to Chimp Eden.

We travelled to other places in Luanda where chimpanzees were being kept. In total we found nine of them, and each location seemed worse than the previous one.

Unfortunately, when we got back to South Africa the relationship between the Swiss experts and the other parties involved in the project deteriorated to the point where they abruptly decided to terminate their contract and go home. I had committed myself to getting all of the chimpanzees out of Luanda but I wasn't going to get very far unless I could find someone with the expertise to finish the facility.

It was a stroke of luck when my mother Marina made contact with Phillip Cronje from the Johannesburg Zoo. My mother is a skilled builder and had been working on the building designs with Eric on a daily basis. Her chance discussion with Phillip culminated in him resigning from his post as head primate curator at the zoo and replacing Eric as the sanctuary manager.

It was a great relief for all of us to have on board a South African with more than twenty-eight years' experience of primate caretaking. And not only did he communicate well with everyone, but he had a level-headed approach to solving the construction design challenges. He was the right person for me to learn from – and I didn't have to wait long.

TWO

WALK THE WALK,
TALK THE TALK

At the end of December 2005 I had my first opportunity to work hands-on with a chimpanzee. After our initial visit to Angola to identify chimpanzees for relocation to Chimp Eden, the government of Angola surprised us with a demand for $380 000 which, in their words, 'would be used for other primate conservation initiatives in the Cabinda province of Angola'. Needless to say, this was unacceptable to all at JGI South Africa because it would constitute the 'purchase' of chimpanzees.

The situation on the ground was getting desperate as the caretakers of the chimpanzee Sally couldn't stay in Luanda over the Christmas period and asked Chimp Eden to help solve the problem of finding someone to look after Sally. Naturally, I jumped at the opportunity of getting practical caretaking experience. To be frank, any chimpanzee would have done! There was also the matter of persuading the government to issue the export permits, regardless of their request for funds.

The plan was to send Phillip in ahead of me until such time as I could join him. Responsibilities back at Chimp Eden delayed me for a month and I eventually joined a very lonely Phillip at the Grinaker compound. Although he looked pretty upbeat when I arrived, I knew his time with only a chimpanzee for company couldn't have been easy. Sally, on the other hand, did not mind the limited companionship and charged around the compound as usual, climbing up and down the few scattered trees.

The compound was vacant of pretty much all of its residents, apart from one or two families that had opted to stay behind during the Christmas break. It was remarkable how similar the compound was to a typical American-style suburb with its wooden box-like houses, each having either two or three bedrooms and a small unattended garden. The houses were all equipped with air conditioning and satellite television and were comfortable to live in compared with anything else Luanda had to offer.

I knew that I had a lot to learn, and having Sally running around without any form of restraint provided the perfect learning ground. The first lesson came around breakfast time on my first day; I had the task of preparing the meal while Phillip tried to occupy Sally and keep her out of the small kitchen. Now and then she managed to slip past him and deliberately grabbed anything she could get her hands on, making off with it through the back door at the speed of lightning. This lasted only as long as it took Phillip to catch up with her, when she dropped whatever she had in order to put as much distance as possible between her and Phillip. There was obviously a lesson to be learned. I mean, how exactly did Phillip manage to get so much respect from her?

The living room in the house had a small dining table with three places, which was quite convenient for us. As Phillip and I sat down for breakfast opposite each other, Sally quietly slipped on to the third vacant chair. She was very respectful when she was so close to Phillip. I asked Phillip what the secret to his success was and he replied, 'They need to know what comes after "the finger".' If you were a child who grew up in a household where discipline was a way of life, you will know that 'the finger' is the way a parent warns a child of a spanking if the bad behaviour continues.

So, Lesson Number One: in order to be able to take care of a chimpanzee, you need to have the respect of the chimpanzee. Obviously, if the chimpanzee got out of line I would, I guess, have to be able to spank the monkey! But this was something I wasn't sure about and quite frankly I wasn't going to try it without some expert assistance. Sally showed no respect for me when Phillip was absent so a showdown with her was inevitable, although I wasn't sure that the one who walked away with the respect would be me.

Sally wasn't allowed to walk around the house without a nappy, although the stains on the furniture told a different story. At breakfast, without warning, my nose was assailed by the stench of fresh poo and it didn't take long for me to figure out that neither Phillip nor I was responsible. Little Sally had innocently crapped in her nappy. Phillip wasn't too amused but he was used to the nappy-changing routine at inconvenient times and he said, quite cheerfully, 'Come on', grabbed Sally by the arm and slung her on to his hip in one smooth movement while heading for the door.

The kitchen door led to an outside washbasin, ideal for urgent 'bomb' disposal situations and Phillip wasted no time in getting her out of the nappy. Like a good student, I also abandoned my breakfast and positioned myself at his side. To be honest, I wasn't keen on the whole nappy-changing business and avoided the task as often as I could, but the job *did* require it of me. What I didn't count on was the overwhelming smell that hit my nasal cavity as the nappy came off!

Lesson Number Two presented itself.

'You'd better get used to it if you want to work with chimpanzees,' said Phillip. 'I guess it helps if you've had to raise a few kids. The worst comes when they start eating meat.'

This was too much information for me. 'Give me a break, will you?' I said, stepping back a few paces until I could muster the courage to move back to his side again.

Phillip most definitely earned his merit badge after a lifetime of cleaning up chimp poo at the zoo, never mind raising two kids at home. I'd have had to develop a more resistant nose if I'd been in his shoes.

Sally, now accustomed to this unnatural routine, lay on her back looking quite relaxed and watching the proceedings with great amusement. The quality of nappy, though, was not of the best and Phillip was having a hard time trying to fix the sticky little straps of the clean nappy in order to secure it properly. I have a vivid memory of Sally trying to grab her foot with her left arm, probably because she was bored, and me instinctively trying to stop her from doing so, so that she didn't hamper Phillip's efforts. Not realising that I was treading on thin ice, I was watching Phillip's actions instead of Sally's reaction. Quicker than lightning, she grabbed my hand and pulled it towards her mouth while making a horrible shrieking vocalisation. It's funny how moments like these get burned into your memory. I will never forget how one of Sally's canine teeth pierced the skin on my hand, penetrating deep into the flesh. The force of the bite was so intense that it could easily have robbed me of a finger. I didn't try to pull my hand away; I just stared with slow disbelief at what was happening. She let go of my hand and Phillip pulled her off the table and took her into the house, still uttering warning vocalisations. I could not quite accept what my eyes were telling me – she had bitten a hole almost clean through my hand! There was no blood at first, just a gaping hole, which brings me to Lesson Number Three: never take your eyes off the chimp. I didn't need Phillip to tell me this: I had learned the hard way.

I went over to the washbasin, opened the tap and started cleaning my hand under a stream of cold water. Phillip eventually came out of the house with Sally on his hip, giving no clue as to why they had rushed inside or why Sally was now so calm.

I wasn't mad at all but I still had to ask: 'What the hell did I do wrong?'

Phillip walked towards me, bringing Sally up close. 'Show her your hand.'

Not wanting a repeat of the incident, I looked at him in amazement. 'No, thank you.'

He chuckled and repeated: 'Just show her your hand.'

I removed my hand from under the tap and slowly brought it up to Sally's eye level, all the while watching her closely. She slowly took hold of my hand, brought it right up to her nose and sniffed at it. It will never cease to amaze me how much emotion chimpanzees can convey. With eyes drooping and flattened lips and a slight *'hoo hoo hoo'* she looked incredibly sorry for what she had done. Phillip looked at me and then back down at Sally.

'Never hold a grudge,' he said. 'One minute they bite your fingers off and the next they expect you to groom them.' Lesson Number Four.

I had learned four of the most important rules about working with chimpanzees in the space of less than an hour. If this was what it was going to be like working around chimpanzees, then my life was going to be anything but boring! The rest of the day was uneventful as it mostly involved trying to find a rare commodity in Luanda: a Band-Aid.

I had arrived one day ahead of the New Year's Eve celebrations and I was determined to show Phillip and Sally a good time since they had been isolated for so long. It was to be a barbecue, a couple of beers for the humans, and good company – to remind Phillip what was waiting for him back home. It had to be a night to remember. And it certainly was – only that had not so much to do with my plans as with Sally's misbehaviour.

The next day Phillip, Sally and I drove around Luanda gathering all the ingredients we needed for our party. Around 7pm the community hall, which was located about fifty feet from our house, was transformed from a deserted building into a rowdy festive gathering that could probably be heard all the way to South Africa.

Trying to keep Sally at our barbecue outside our house was like trying to keep Paris Hilton away from a nightclub. Impossible! She kept making her way across to the hall and we kept following in an attempt to keep her under control. Her first act of sabotage was to grab a bowl filled with punch and make her way to the only place we couldn't follow: up the nearest tall tree. She was aware that she was behaving very badly and relished the annoyance of the partygoers. Many were ready to string her up and my negotiation skills had never been more needed. Eventually a truce was called, the terms of which were that if Sally made any further attempts at stealing booze physical assault would be unavoidable.

We came up with the following plan. We would ignore her completely, as though the bowl of punch had not been missed, but this just made Sally even more malicious. To my great relief, she let the bowl go, but this was only because she was done with her warm-up and was moving on to the main show. She chose the biggest guy in the room, lifted his vodka punch mix and ran back up the tree vocalising warning calls all the while. This didn't go down well with the big guy. Neither Phillip nor I felt like an argument so once again we pleaded with Sally to come down out of the tree. The punch jug was filled to the brim and it must have taken every ounce of skill for Sally to perform such a star balancing act without spilling so much as a drop. But our entreaties fell on deaf ears as Sally slowly started to consume the punch. The furious owner of the jug, threatening to do serious harm to Sally, now started directing his anger towards Phillip and me. While we tried to explain chimpanzee behaviour to this menacing man, Sally managed to drink the entire gallon of punch.

Fortunately, some of the other partygoers urged the man to abandon his rant and return to the festivities. Throwing up his arms, he eventually turned his back on us and walked off muttering, 'Get your chimp under control or I will!'

I looked at Phillip. 'That was close,' I said, with an uneasy chuckle. We both knew that if Sally did any more thieving we would have to make for the hills.

Sally, now perched on the very end of the highest branch, looked as though she was going to pass out at any moment and fall out of the tree. Phillip and I reacted at the same time, rushing to the base of the tree and yelling at her to wake up. Falling from the tree would surely result in injury to Sally whose chosen branch was more than twenty feet from the ground. Sally barely reacted to our yelling, her eyelids fluttering open briefly and then closing again. But she could no longer keep hold of the glass jug and it took clever footwork and my best ball sense to catch it.

Our yelling at Sally attracted the attention of some of the partying people who realised that Sally was completely intoxicated. Finding this amusing, some of them walked up to the tree and joined in our yelling, followed by raucous laughter. After a while Sally opened her eyes and started to position herself for the descent, slipping and sliding and missing half the branches she should have held on to. Phillip and I were both ready to catch her as she fell out of the tree.

'Show's over, folks,' I muttered, leaving it to Phillip to carry Sally home. I returned the jug and apologised for the inconvenience our chimpanzee had caused. Her final antics had lightened the atmosphere somewhat.

As I walked into the house, Phillip said, 'She's sleeping like a baby.'

We shared a good laugh about the disastrous evening. My plans might have been completely ruined but it was certainly a New Year's Eve I wouldn't forget any time soon.

The next two weeks were spent taking care of Sally and travelling to the other sites where chimpanzees were being kept. One in particular was not looking too good; his name was Zac and he was a nineteen-year-old who was chained to a tree outside a nightclub. I had visited this site on my earlier trip in September and even then I had said to myself that he was probably beyond help. I'd estimated that he weighed about 35 pounds, which was shocking considering that a male chimpanzee of his age was supposed to weigh in the order of 120 to 145 pounds. The site had a lane of trees, each about 20 feet high, separated from the nightclub by what looked like a horse riding enclosure about 160 feet in diameter. There were three chimpanzees in all, chained to every other tree, with Zac right at the end.

According to the owner, a Mr Neves, the chimpanzees were separated to prevent them from getting entangled in one another's chains. To me this was a terribly sad situation because they are such social creatures. Indeed, during my limited observations of these chimps I saw them trying to interact several times only to be thwarted by the chains which did not allow them to get to within more than a few inches of one another.

Zac was the eldest of the three chimps and he was in a shocking condition. According to visitors, he was showing symptoms of malaria, and this wasn't the first time. It was distressing for me to see him crawling under a blanket in temperatures well above 30°C. How he had survived chained to a tree for such a long time defied the imagination. How anyone was capable of inflicting this sort of cruelty on an animal was beyond my comprehension and made me extremely angry.

Zac's survival could probably be attributed to regular visits by caring individuals, expatriates who visited the site only to bring medicine, food and water and, most importantly, social interaction. I could imagine that Zac was becoming increasingly aggressive and frustrated with his environment, especially since he was denied any socialising with animals that were literally only inches away from him. Interaction with human visitors was dangerous, but I think it was what saved him. Lucinda Piets was an Australian expat who did her best to interact with Zac and somehow navigated the hazards without losing a limb. Her regular visits ensured that he had some social interaction, and she was smart enough to sense when he was becoming aggressive and managed to avoid injury.

It was rumoured that many other animals had come and gone from this place of abuse, so how was it that Zac had managed to survive? Can it be that some animals are mentally stronger than others, or are the efforts of a handful of humans sufficient perhaps to give them a reason to live?

I knew that if it was possible to get Zac out of Angola and to Chimpanzee Eden he could be saved with proper medical treatment, but the lack of response from the Angolan government did not hold much promise for his future. I had sent more than twenty faxes to Dr Almeida and to his superior and hoped that their reason for not answering me was a broken fax machine rather than their choosing to ignore me.

One day I was woken by the blistering heat of the Angolan morning sun. With sweat already starting to stain my clothes, I lay in bed pondering our predicament. I had been in Angola for more than a month, Phillip for two. Surely this could not continue indefinitely? My thoughts turned into frustration that built up to a point where I knew that taking action was the only way to sort out the situation. I confronted Phillip, who was already up and filling his role of play partner to Sally.

'I can't take this shit any more! I'm going to call Dr Almeida again and if he refuses to talk to me, then I say we march down to his office and give him an ultimatum. Either he gives us the export permit or we dump Sally on his desk for him to take care of.'

He surprised me with his answer. 'Let's go.'

That's what I like about Phillip – he gets straight to the point. Of course neither of us intended leaving Sally with Almeida but it would be a powerful way of perhaps jolting him into action that would ultimately see all the chimps being issued with export permits and leaving Luanda.

I walked out of the house pulling my Thuraya satellite phone from my side pocket and dialled Almeida's office number. Pacing up and down the dry grass of the lawn, I waited anxiously for the phone to be answered. After only a few seconds a voice crackled on the other end of the line.

'Bon dia.'

'Yes, good morning. Who am I speaking to?'

'This is Oliveira speaking.'

I had no quarrel with Dr Almeida's second in command. In truth, I think he was also a slave to the bureaucratic nightmare that was keeping us in Luanda. If I had an ally in the ministry of forestry, it was him. Always polite and accommodating, he was a rare person in this part of the world.

'Oliveira! Nice to speak to you, my friend. But we have a serious problem, Oliveira. We have been looking after Sally for a long time now and we are getting nowhere with the export permit. The owners are not here at the house and we cannot continue to stay here babysitting indefinitely. You must tell Dr Almeida that we need the permit now. Otherwise we will have no option but to leave the chimpanzee at your office.'

The message was blunt and hopefully Oliveira would be able to communicate our desperation to his superior before we got to the office.

'I understand. I will tell Dr Almeida about your problem.'

'Can I come to your office to see him?'

'You may come at any time, you are always welcome.'

'Okay. I will be there as soon as possible.'

'Okay, okay. I will tell Dr Almeida you are coming. You are welcome,' he said before ending the call.

We did not waste any time. Phillip slapped a nappy on to Sally, who was just about to start her after-breakfast routine of rampaging around the complex, and we climbed into the vehicle which was on loan to us from Grinaker and set off for the ministry.

With most of the expatriates away for the holidays, the drivers employed by Grinaker had not much to do and access to them and a vehicle was relatively easy. Phillip sat in the back of the vehicle with Sally while I sat up front impatiently explaining to the driver where we wanted to go. As we drove out of the gate of the complex I suddenly doubted the sanity of my actions. I mean, it is one thing making brave talk in the company of your friends, but quite another walking into the office of a senior government official with a string of demands. Things did not often work out well for a white man in dark Africa who adopted this kind of attitude, but my reasoning was simple: do this now or risk being stuck in Angola for who knew how long. How badly can it possibly go, right?

The traffic was surprisingly easy going, although there was the occasional bewildered stare from people unaccustomed to seeing a chimpanzee riding in the back of a vehicle. The ministry's U-shaped building was enormous in relation to the surrounding structures and was easy to find. It was, however, difficult to find parking in its quite extensive parking area. There seemed to be a lot of vehicles there, many of them covered in thick dust as though they had not been moved for years.

The dust-covered vehicles unleashed unsettling thoughts about what might have happened to their owners. Had they made demands on government officials? I have always had a vivid imagination. I removed these ridiculous ideas from my mind, gathered myself together and climbed out of the vehicle as soon as we found a parking bay. Phillip was quick to follow and Sally was behaving quite well.

We passed through the rather dull lobby and went straight to a noticeboard to look up the floor on which we would find the ministry. Satisfied, I led the way up to the second floor with Phillip and Sally close behind.

Arriving on the second floor, we walked through the glass doors that separated the stairs from a narrow passage off which individual offices opened. I wasn't sure which way to go, so I entered the first office with an open door. It was full of people – about seven or so, sitting at desks and staring at us with expressions of disbelief all over their faces. I was sure I wasn't the first white man to set foot in the building and was puzzled by the way they were gaping at us. As I opened my mouth to speak to them it occurred to me that Sally was the likely reason for their expressions but I carried on waving my hand to attract their attention and saying slowly and carefully, as though addressing someone who was hard of hearing, 'Does anybody know where the office of Dr Almeida is?'

The lack of response in any language probably meant that English was non-existent here, but the name seemed to do the trick as one of the ladies got up from her desk and tried to squeeze past me through the narrow doorway. As she did this Sally erupted and lunged forward lightly scratching the lady's face and uttering a warning bark that could have raised the roof.

'*Oohhoo-oohoooo-ooohhooo!*'

It was enough to give one a fright even if one was anticipating it and, not surprisingly, the somewhat overweight lady was so shocked that she stumbled and fell on to her backside, releasing a retaliatory scream as though she'd been beset by an attack dog rather than an innocent baby chimpanzee.

'Aaaggghhhhh!'

Her screaming re-energised Sally who responded with more warning barks. Phillip tried to restrain Sally, pulling her close to his chest, turning away and yelling at her: 'Sally, no!'

It was a surreal situation which I might have found quite comical at a different time and place, but it really was no laughing matter. People started pouring out of their offices to see what was going on and it was becoming painfully obvious that things were only going to get worse. I tried to downplay the situation by helping the lady to her feet and saying soothingly, 'It's okay, she just wants to play.'

Unfortunately, my attempts to be a convincing liar couldn't transcend the language barrier; no one could understand a word I was saying. As I was helping the lady to her feet two highly polished black shoes appeared in front of me. I looked up into Almeida's face. Nothing really prepares you for a moment like this and he wasn't going to give me a chance to explain. Looking irritated and angry, he motioned towards his office with his left hand.

Things were not going well at all and it was becoming clear that I would have to pull the proverbial rabbit out of a hat in order to save the day. Visibly upset, Almeida walked to his desk and sat down behind it, pointing to the chairs in front of it.

'Sit down!'

I had lost any high ground I might have had and since I was now at a disadvantage I changed my tactics, trying to be cordial and less insistent than I had intended.

'I am sorry to barge in like this,' I said, 'but really we had no other choice. You see, the owners of the chimpanzee had to go back to South

Africa because they had visa problems and so we had to come and take care of Sally. I did mention this in the faxes I have been sending you.' I pointed at the fax machine on his desk.

'You are not supposed to be here. We have an official process.'

An uncomfortable silence followed as I realised where this was going.

'I'm sorry, but we didn't have any other option. The own …'

But before I could finish my sentence he pointed at Sally and then back at me and barked, 'The owners are responsible for the chimpanzee and they must take care of it, not you! You said to Oliveira that you would leave the chimpanzee here if you did not get the export permit. You *do not* tell us what to do. I will tell you how it works in my country!'

A knot had formed at the back of my throat and my heart sank.

'You take the chimpanzee back to the house where you found it and you go back to South Africa *now* or I put you in jail!' He managed to slow down the word 'now' with great effect.

I mustered up the guts to say, 'But what are we supposed to do? There is nobody to take care of the chimp.'

He motioned towards the door and snapped, 'Leave!'

I stared at him, refusing to break eye contact, and I could feel my blood pressure rising. I wanted to jump across the desk and throttle him. In fact, if Phillip hadn't been there I would probably have done exactly that and would certainly have been thrown in jail.

'Come on, Eugene, let's go.'

We got up without saying another word and left the room. My mind was racing. What was I going to do now? I knew that Almeida was not joking; he would make good on his promise to throw me in jail even if it was only to prove a point.

I got into the front passenger seat of the vehicle and slammed the door, cursing loudly. The full extent of our predicament had yet to sink in. This wasn't my country, yet I was stuck here doing a job that Almeida and his people were supposed to be doing.

Almeida was right in a way: I shouldn't be here, but nor should Sally. Her expatriate owners had negotiated for her with a restaurant owner who used her as an attraction for patrons, their sole intention being to save her from a life of misery. Neither of us should be here.

The driver stared at me in confusion until Phillip calmly said, 'Camp, camp, por favor.'

The driver nodded and started the car. Gazing out of the window at nothing in particular, all I could think of was kicking Almeida's behind. Little was said on the way back to the house until Phillip finally broke the silence. 'That guy is an idiot and there is nothing you can do about it.' Phillip, level-headed as always.

I turned to look at Phillip and Sally's innocent little face caught my eye. 'At least you provided the laugh of the day,' I said and we both burst out laughing. But our sombre mood returned as the reality of our situation hit home. There was no one to take care of Sally in our absence and it would be at least another two weeks before the South African owners returned to Angola.

That night was one of the most restless I can remember. As I tossed and turned I knew that if I couldn't come up with a solution Sally would face an uncertain future. I even considered smuggling Sally across the

Namibian border which, of course, would be totally illegal. I always make a point of exploring every possible escape route when I'm in a strange country. The journey by road to the Namibian border would take about six days by taxi, so the fact that I was even considering this meant that I really was out of options.

Not getting an export permit was a worst-case scenario which we discussed unendingly, and euthanasia was one of the realistic options. Just thinking about it made my blood run cold. Would I be capable of doing such a thing? I didn't think so. I needed a workable solution that would buy us enough time to bring international pressure to bear on the Angolans. And then I had a 'eureka' moment. The solution had pretty much been staring me in the face every day: our driver. He was a well-spoken man who had enjoyed interacting with Sally on a few occasions. If we could teach him the basics of chimp care, we'd have a solution, theoretically at any rate, until the owners returned to Grinaker.

I ran the idea past Phillip and the driver, whose name was Billa. We would of course have to pay him for his services, but that was more than acceptable considering the alternatives. Billa would have to pass a crash course in chimp caretaking which, judging from my own experience, wasn't going to be a walk in the park. But we had no choice and we would have to work fast as the next available flight back to South Africa left in two days' time and Almeida would be watching.

We decided that the best way to teach Billa every possible contingency was for the four of us to lock ourselves in the house with no way of escape. This was an interesting prospect. If I had learned anything at that point it was that Sally was a complete nightmare inside the house.

And so we went into the house, locking both the front and back doors. The living room was pretty small with one standard uncomfortable chair, a small couch and the dining table that seated three people. The television in the corner would help relieve the boredom – but then again taking care of Sally was no boring task.

As we got started Billa took the chair closest to the front door and Sally immediately pounced on him. In general, chimps seem to be attracted to new faces, as if they know they'll have a chance at manipulation. During the few weeks that I had worked with Sally I had had ample opportunity to reinforce my dominance and so keep her under control. Billa did not have this advantage and Sally instinctively focused on him, ignoring both Phillip and me. Her technique was simple: she walked up to him and stretched out her arms towards him as if asking for a hug. Billa was naturally happy with this friendly reception. Playfully, she slowly tested the limits of Billa's tolerance at every opportunity, pulling one of his hands into her mouth and biting down on it. This behaviour intensified until he finally got up and warned her: 'Sally, no!'

But you had to say it like you meant it, otherwise Sally just became more determined. As Billa sat down again Sally pounced once more. Now and then I tried to intervene, grabbing her by the leg as she sped towards him and Phillip warned her from his seat at the table with an occasional 'Saaallly!' accompanied by the 'finger' warning. But there is no way around the fact that sooner or later one had to show dominance and Billa knew this because we kept reminding him. It wasn't long before the inevitable happened. Sally bit down on his hand so hard that he yelled with pain, jerked his arm away and slapped her lightly on the back of her head with his other hand. Then he got up from his chair to demonstrate a more dominant presence.

'Show her the finger!' Phillip cried sensing that this was an ideal opportunity for the lesson.

'Sally, don't do that again!' Billa admonished, eyeballing her and wagging his index finger.

He'd mastered that lesson perfectly. Sally backed away from him with a pitiful expression on her face and immediately stretched out her arm to him.

'Hoo-hoo-hooo,' she wailed, showing her teeth and looking up at him. She had clearly got the message but was now looking for reassurance. 'Okay, pick her up,' Phillip said.

Billa bent over and swooped her up on to his hip and she instantly calmed down.

'You've got it, man!' I proclaimed excitedly. I felt positive for the first time since I'd walked out of Almeida's office.

Phillip or I still handled the nappy changes as we were both worried that there might be a repeat of what had happened to me.

The two days of training were over in no time and, before we knew it, the morning of our departure arrived. In a nutshell, this was the situation: Billa would move into the house, make Sally's baby formula milk three times a day and give her fruit to her heart's content. She would be outside most of the time which eliminated the need for frequent nappy changing.

Billa seemed to be okay with his responsibilities and we both felt as confident as we could be in the circumstances. The only problem was that Sally still slept in Phillip's bed, always clutching his shirt with one hand before she fell asleep. In order to leave the house Phillip needed to get away from her without waking her. If she did wake up and realised that he was leaving we might not be able to get away from her without causing major drama. Because of this, we had come up with a plan. Since she was more dependent on Phillip he would leave first and I would take his place in the bed beside her. The luggage would already be outside the house so noise would be minimal.

At 4am I made my way to Phillip's room and opened the door. Phillip, lying beside Sally, was already dressed and ready to go. I deferred asking him how he had managed that, leaving it as a topic of conversation on the flight home. Sally, who was snoozing comfortably, had positioned herself at the foot of the bed with her head pointing away from the door. I gave Phillip a thumbs-up and lay down on the bed beside Sally. As he closed the door Sally lifted her head and slowly looked around. When she noticed that the person lying beside her was not Phillip she freaked out. Jumping off the bed she ran frantically through the small house checking each room and vocalising her distress. She made her way to the window and looked outside, scanning the area around the house from side to side. But she could not see Phillip and once the idea that he was gone sank in she jumped back on to the bed next to me. I suppose she reckoned that I was the next best thing. Over the last month I had grown quite fond of Sally and I'd like to think that the feeling was mutual.

I tried my best to calm her down. 'Ssshhh … it's going to be okay. He'll be back soon,' I said, knowing full well that this might have been the last time she would ever see Phillip.

Sally stared at me as if looking for a definitive answer as to Phillip's whereabouts. What if she didn't go back to sleep? We were running out of time to get to the airport, and Almeida's threats were very much on my mind. The sun was not up yet and the only light outside was from the street lamps. An hour passed before Sally finally rested her head on the bed. Still not taking her eyes off me she clutched my shirt tightly. Then her eyes started drooping with tiredness and it wasn't much longer before she was asleep. It was now or never. I gently loosened her grip on my shirt and placed her hand on the bed beside me. She didn't seem to notice.

I got up slowly and tiptoed out of the room and then out of the house where Billa was waiting patiently.

'Okay, boet, good luck,' I whispered and he acknowledged me with a simple nod. Then he walked through the open doorway and softly closed the door behind him. It seemed rather too easy. Not wanting to tempt fate, I quickly made my way towards Phillip who was standing under a lone street lamp at the end of the road. We thought it wisest to board our taxi out of sight of the house.

The cool morning air was tainted by the smell of burning fires. We weren't the only ones up at the crack of dawn; for most people in Luanda a fire was the only means of cooking a meal or making a hot drink before leaving for work. I looked towards the hillside, scanning for the sun that was about to rise. I was halfway to the taxi when a loud yell pierced the morning silence. Sally had discovered my deception and was calling hysterically from inside the house. Even though I had no children at that stage, it sure felt as though I was abandoning one. Every bone in my body wanted to react to the desperate cry of the chimp who regarded me more as a parent than a caretaker.

I stopped, overtaken with numbness. I should have kept on walking, but I allowed myself to look back at the house. Sally's calls had become even louder; they resonated through the quiet Grinaker compound becoming even more insistent as panic set in. I took a deep breath and tried to relax, but I couldn't stop the wave of emotion that made my eyes fill with tears. I had had no idea it was going to be this hard. Somehow, this little creature had crept into my heart and it was hard to let go. Time was passing and we had to leave. I began walking towards the taxi again, Sally's desperate calls ringing in my ears. As I reached the taxi I made myself a promise: I would be back for her, even if it meant risking jail or life itself.

THREE

LEBANON –
NO PLACE LIKE HOME

Within two weeks of our departure from Luanda Sally's owners arrived back to relieve Billa of his caretaking duties. There was still no word from Dr Almeida on whether or not export permits for the chimps would be issued. The efforts in Angola now moved from caretaking to applying pressure on the ministry with the support of the international community. JGI South Africa also sent in volunteers from time to time to help with Sally, as taking care of her was turning into a full-time undertaking and placing immense strain on her owners.

At this time I was introduced by Doug Cress, executive director of the Pan African Sanctuary Alliance, to a man named Mark Lane, a self-proclaimed great ape activist who worked for a prominent activist in Kenya.

I never learned the reasons why Mark, who was born in the USA, became an activist in Africa. Nevertheless, he was spearheading an investigation into the illegal trade in great apes in the Middle East – more specifically in Lebanon. It seemed that with the help of the Lebanese department of environmental affairs he had managed to obtain orders to confiscate illegally held chimpanzees in Beirut, the capital of Lebanon. Needless to say, we heeded Mark's call for assistance and reassured Doug that we would be doing so. Our directive was limited to the relocation of the primates, and not any of the secondary tasks such as the arrangement of permits, negotiations, transport and so on.

What made this project really exciting was that we now had adult chimpanzees to focus on – experience I really needed. I had spent a lot of time around Sally and other Angolan chimpanzees, but I wasn't quite ready to tackle the relocation of two adult chimpanzees and one juvenile from a country that I had never visited before. I set about preparing for the mission by focusing on the logistics. We would require strong but lightweight crates and, to my surprise, I could not source a single crate from any zoo in South Africa. It seemed that quite a few zoos did have primates but none of them had bothered to keep their travel crates, if they had had any to begin with. I obtained specifications from the Air Transport Association and contracted a builder to get to work building the crates. It wasn't long before we had six crates ready for transport. I thought it best that we build extra crates while we were about it, in the event that we were called upon to move more chimpanzees.

What I did find incredibly challenging was finding the expertise to assist me in finding out about the whole importation process. Working between the different government departments that we would require authorisation from, I pieced together a rough idea of what was needed.

The CITES import permit would come from our provincial CITES wildlife authority; the blood import permit would then be sourced from the state veterinary department which would, incidentally, only be issued if we used a South African veterinarian to take multiple blood samples for analysis. The blood would then be sent to a laboratory in The Netherlands for analysis and the results would be faxed to the South African state veterinarian. The chimpanzees' blood would be tested for the Marburg, Ebola and Simian AIDS viruses. After testing, however, the results would have to be confirmed by the state veterinarian in the country of export. If this sounds confusing to you, believe me, it is!

After export the primates were to travel to the quarantine accommodation located at Chimpanzee Eden where they would have to spend a period of no less than three months. Our earlier expert, Eric du Bois, had recognised the importance of a proper quarantine facility and his design was one of the first to be commissioned at Chimpanzee Eden at the beginning of 2005.

When we received the export permits from Mark we arranged for the crates to be flown to Beirut on a commercial cargo flight, and then Phillip and I boarded a plane for Beirut on 25 February 2006. We would have a six-hour stopover in Dubai before catching a connecting flight to Beirut. Everything had gone well so far and I had a hard time containing my excitement, knowing that in a few hours we would be part of an effort to confiscate adult chimpanzees and relocate them to a new life.

We duly landed at Beirut's Rafic Hariri International Airport and made our way to passport control and Customs clearance. Armed security personnel were very visible, which should have served as a warning of things to come. As we reached the front of the queue I was asked to hand our passports to an official whose attitude suggested that he had a general lack of enthusiasm for his job. He motioned with one hand, took both our passports, and then pointed towards the line on the floor behind which I was apparently required to remain. Painfully slowly, he paged through my passport, studying the contents as though he was looking for something other than the visa we had obtained at the Lebanese consulate in South Africa. After some time he looked at the 'new arrivals' form that we had had to fill in on the flight, studying its contents with an expression of concern on his face.

'Who arranged for your invitation to Lebanon?' he asked. As with the residents of many other African countries, we required an invitation from a local company or individual to visit Lebanon.

'Our contact person is Alissa Khoury; we are here to help with an animal welfare case.' I pointed towards the space on the form where I had filled in Alissa's name.

Not amused at seeing that I had again crossed the line on the floor, he said: 'Yes, but who does she work for? What is her telephone number? Where are you going to stay?'

'Sorry,' I replied. 'I probably forgot to fill that in on the form. May I have it back, please.' Expressionlessly, he handed me the form and slumped back into his chair.

I took a moment to find Alissa's number on my phone and wrote down a description of the non-profit company BETA, the acronym for the organisation called Beirut for the Ethical Treatment of Animals.

He studied the new information for a moment or two then motioned to another official who was leaning against the wall behind him. The man came over and after exchanging a few words in Arabic he took the form. He then made a phone call, looking at me suspiciously from time to time. Although I couldn't put my finger on it, something about us had raised their suspicions – I couldn't imagine every new arrival in the country being subjected to such close scrutiny. After about five minutes the second man returned, mumbled something to the first official who was still slumped in his chair with his arms crossed.

'Have you ever been to Israel?' I was asked.

With a puzzled look on my face, I replied, 'No, not that I know of.'

The attempt at humour did not have the desired effect, but the official gestured that Phillip and I should proceed along the narrow passage.

'What was that all about?' I asked Phillip over my shoulder.

'Maybe they just don't like guys wearing khaki,' he answered.

'Or maybe we look too much like Yanks.'

As we entered the crowded arrivals area I scanned the front row of onlookers who were held back by a rope barrier. Then I noticed a dark-haired young woman on one side who was holding up a piece of white cardboard with the words 'Mr Cousins' on it.

'Close enough,' I thought.

Approaching her, I said, 'Hi, I'm Eugene ... are you Alissa?'

'No, I'm Monique,' she said, giving me a warm smile and shaking my hand and pointing towards Alissa who was standing a little way away.

'Just follow me,' she said as she fought her way through the crowd.

With Phillip following close behind we walked around the barrier and followed Monique. She was heading towards two people who were engaged in an intense conversation. Alissa was also a short, dark-haired girl in her early twenties; the two girls looked as though they could be twins. Alissa looked upset, her conversation with the man was quite heated and I got the impression that something was wrong.

The man was Mark Lane. He looked as though he was in his late twenties, or perhaps early thirties, and had long hair and his pale skin was sunburnt to a painful looking red.

'Hi, I'm Eugene and this is Phillip.' We shook hands.

'I'm Mark … saw you guys on the flight, but wasn't certain it was you.'

'I am Alissa,' said the second dark-haired girl.

A short uncomfortable silence followed. Not wanting to beat about the bush, I said, '*So*, what's going on?'

'The chimps are gone,' said Alissa shrugging her shoulders and lifting her hands palms upwards. This was a bombshell of note, and one that none of us were willing to accept, especially since we'd just arrived.

'You are kidding, right?' I looked at them in turn.

'Afraid not,' Mark said without showing any emotion. 'The owners must have been warned about the confiscation.'

I wasn't sure what annoyed me more – the fact that the mission was already bust, or the fact that Mark was being so cool about it. If it had been my mission I would have freaked out, to say the least.

Over the next few days I would get to know Mark pretty well, especially his remarkable ability to say everything in the same tone of voice and with an expression that showed absolutely no emotion. Did he know that his gift would win him a fortune at the poker tables of Vegas?

I looked at Phillip, who was staring at me over the frames of his spectacles. 'Well, what are we going to do about it?' I asked.

Not having any answers, Alissa motioned towards the exit. 'Why don't we talk about it on the way? We have to go to the police immediately if there's to be any chance of getting the chimps back.'

As we started walking towards the exit, Phillip finally asked the question that was on everyone's mind. 'What exactly do you mean by *disappeared?*'

'We sent people this morning to two of the three locations to see if the chimps were still there … and they were both gone. The restaurant, Mr Steak, owned by a Mr Naifeh and Hamieh Gaz owned by, yes, you've guessed it, a Mr Hamieh.'

As he got into the front passenger seat Mark remarked, 'We do however think that the infant chimpanzee is still at the zoo facility so there might be a chance that it wasn't removed.' This evidently was information passed on by Alissa during the conversation they were having before we arrived.

'I take it we are heading for the police station to get the confiscation enforced?' I said, as I stared through the windshield at the road ahead.

'Yes,' Mark and Alissa replied simultaneously.

'If the young chimp is still at the zoo, will we need one of the crates, Phil?' I asked.

'Well, if it's an infant I don't think we should be wasting any time. We could just go to the safe house as soon as we've got the chimp and pick up a crate later.'

'The crates are still at the airline cargo department,' Alissa said, glancing over her shoulder.

Not having the crates ready meant that we would not be able to rescue any of the other chimps in the event that things changed dramatically. We were all in agreement that time was of the essence and that the best chance of saving at least one of the chimpanzees would be to go and look for the one at the zoo as soon as possible.

Not much else was said on the drive to the police station. It didn't make sense to me that the chimps could simply disappear, but then I was new to this part of the world. At the back of my mind I started having doubts about Mark, who was the one who had arranged the whole mission. I didn't know much about him besides the fact that he was an American living in Kenya with his employer and that he was involved in investigations into the illegal trade in endangered species in the Middle East, although I did not know what the full extent of his role was.

But then Mark was solely responsible for this mission. He had done the investigation and had hidden camera footage that directly implicated a pet shop trader. So I erased my unjustifiable doubts from my mind and looked out the window at the buildings we were passing by. They looked like small apartment blocks. The traffic was pretty disorganised, the streets were dusty and odd bits of litter fluttered around. It was a whole new world to me. I considered myself a seasoned traveller but I had never been to the Middle East before and it all looked very different. I couldn't help but wonder why chimpanzees had landed up here in the first place. The CITES restrictions placed a pretty tight lid on the movement of endangered species, especially species like chimps and gorillas which drew a lot of attention, yet reports were rife about private collections that included both of these species. Lebanon was obviously not a range state for the great apes, and nor was it close to one.

To satisfy my curiosity, I asked, 'Mark, where were the chimpanzees smuggled from?'

'They were most likely smuggled in through airport Customs,' he replied. 'It's my belief that there is a corrupt Customs official who is allowing them through. I'm not sure exactly how the trade works, but you can order a chimp at almost any pet shop here ... different ages, different genders, different prices – anything from three thousand to twenty thousand dollars.'

'Jeezzz,' Phillip whistled in amazement.

'The most likely place they are smuggling them from is Nigeria,' Mark continued. 'I exposed a syndicate that tries to sell Nigerian chimps in Cairo and I'm pretty sure that these chimps here come from the same place.'

'Why would anyone here want to own a chimpanzee – what reason?' I asked.

'A lot of rich guys here are looking to brag about the fact that they have a chimpanzee as well as other exotic species such as tigers. And, like the chimps we want to rescue, they are also used to attract and entertain people ... one location is a fuel station, another is a restaurant.'

This reminded me of Zac and the two other chimpanzees with him in Angola. The nightclub owner had also used them for entertainment, allegedly giving them cigarettes and alcohol, hoping that the effects of these would amuse his patrons.

When we arrived at the police station Alissa and Mark went in to seek the cooperation of the police in enforcing the confiscation while the rest of us opted to stay in the vehicle. More than an hour passed before they returned. I imagined they were having to deal with the type of officialdom that likes to drag proceedings down with unnecessary bureaucratic red tape. But when they did arrive back they had good news.

'The police realise the importance of moving fast on the case and have assured us they will meet us outside the zoo facility,' Alissa said in an upbeat tone. 'I've also asked a few of my friends to meet us outside the zoo. They are part of an organisation that people in Beirut respect.'

'Sounds good to me,' I answered optimistically. 'As long as we get the job done.' I glanced at Phillip who was quietly formulating his own opinion.

Things were looking up. Surely it was unlikely that all three chimpanzees could disappear at the same time? The atmosphere in the car was tense but excited. This would be a first for me and I could hardly contain my restlessness.

Alissa brought the vehicle to a stop in an open parking lot that was totally devoid of other vehicles. Phillip and I scanned the surroundings, looking for any clues of captive animals.

'The zoo is just across the bridge,' Alissa said, pointing at the road ahead of us.

Animal City Zoo and its adjacent parking lot was situated alongside a gorgeous river with a huge cliff on the opposite side that channelled the massive flow of water. We all disembarked and I walked up to the barrier, taking a moment to enjoy the view of the fast-flowing river. The empty parking lot and the eerie silence raised the level of tension in the air. After a few minutes a silver 740i BMW with dark tinted windows entered the parking lot and came to a halt next to our vehicle. The passenger side window rolled down revealing a gentleman of Middle Eastern descent. Alissa walked up to the window and talked to him briefly. The man just nodded his head in agreement. Who he was, was none of our business as Phillip and I were responsible only for the relocation of the chimps and not for any other arrangements. Eventually the occupants got out of their car and gathered around the vehicle where Alissa introduced them to Mark and Phillip. I walked back and introduced myself to them, shaking their hands. I wasn't one for formalities but I didn't want to be impolite either.

'Eugene and Phillip, they are from South Africa,' Alissa said.

'Salim,' one man said with a slight grin. The second man simply nodded. I remember thinking that there was something odd about these guys. They didn't look much like tree huggers to me.

They directed their attention at Alissa, continuing their conversation in Arabic. Impoliteness is one thing but feeling like a wall painting is another so I gestured to Phillip to follow me. When we reached the barrier I asked: 'So, what's the plan?'

'I don't know. But I think we let them take care of the business side of things and once they give us the go-ahead we just try and keep the chimp as calm as possible. It shouldn't be too difficult with an infant. The main thing is to get into the car as quickly as possible because the chimp will be freaked out with all these people around and we don't want it to be running off into the hills.'

'We're just going to ride with it in the car?'

'I don't see why not. We did it in Angola.'

'Okay, you're the boss,' I said. 'Nice river, huh?' The rhetorical question was a futile attempt to ease the tension we were both feeling.

We turned to face the party gathered at the cars when a police motorcade of three vehicles came into view. The leading vehicle drew to a halt alongside Alissa, the passenger window rolled down and the occupant barked something at Alissa in Arabic.

'Okay, guys, show time,' she said excitedly.

We hurriedly got back into the vehicle. Alissa drove behind the motorcade with Salim and his companion bringing up the rear. We drove for about 200 yards before the leading car stopped right outside the entrance to the zoo. No fewer than ten officers disembarked from their vehicles, although I must admit that the thought of counting them did not really enter my mind.

Not wanting to get in the way of officialdom, neither Phillip nor I rushed in, giving the police ample time to make their way through the entrance gate. I carried a Sony PD-150 video camera in the bag that was always slung over my shoulder. I checked for a tape and, satisfied, I filmed the zoo entrance. My main reason for bringing a camera was to document as much of what took place as possible, hoping that I would be able to use it when I returned home for the purpose of raising awareness. Even then, I realised that exposure was the key to changing the course of extinction.

Satisfied with my footage, I joined Phillip who was making his way through the gate. Mark had walked straight to the room where the infant chimpanzee was allegedly being kept and from his body language when he emerged I could tell that he had had no joy.

By this time Alissa had dragged the manageress out of her office and together with a police officer they were having a heated debate in Arabic. When we met up with Mark he said, 'The chimp is gone.'

I didn't want to accept this and went into the room to check for myself. The cage where the chimpanzee was supposedly being held was empty.

'Perhaps they are hiding the chimp elsewhere in the zoo,' I said to anyone who was listening.

'Why don't we have a look?' Phillip answered.

The two of us set off in different directions, each hoping that our search would yield some clues as to the whereabouts of the young chimpanzee. The zoo had a main circular walkway with the entrance and exit at the same place. Cages lined both sides of the walkway. At the entrance was a cage with an adult Hamadryas baboon. Encountering primates other than chimpanzees on rescue missions was something I had thought about a lot. Do you only rescue chimpanzees, or do you include other primate species as well? As JGI South Africa we would only be allowed to export chimpanzees. But if the Lebanese department of environmental affairs could be convinced that other species should be confiscated because of valid animal welfare concerns, then, as a secondary objective, we would obviously try to find suitable homes for them. If the management of this particular zoo could prove that it had a CITES import permit for the baby chimp, then we wouldn't be able to confiscate it. An additional problem was that other primate species might not enjoy the same level of protection that CITES affords chimpanzees.

CITES is the acronym for the Convention on International Trade in Endangered Species of Wild Fauna and Flora and it pretty much governs international trade in any endangered species. Although all signatory countries are legally bound by the convention, its terms do not replace the laws of the signatory country. This would come back to haunt us soon enough.

I paused for a second at the cage of the Hamadryas baboon, pitying its miserable existence in this totally unstimulating environment. But for the moment our focus was the chimp and BETA would have to argue a new case for the baboon, if it chose to. I set off again along the circular walkway, scanning each of the cages I passed for any sign of the chimp. The zoo was a deeply depressing place: wolves, bears, lions – all of them wild species that needed open spaces – condemned by humans to this horrid place of confinement.

The most shocking was a cage containing a grizzly bear that was so small that the bear was unable to stand fully upright. I noticed a wolf frantically pacing up and down its cage showing signs of a mental condition known as 'stereotypic behaviour'. Stereotypic behaviour is typically a repetitive behaviour pattern with no obvious function which results from the immense mental suffering experienced by captive animals in a negative environment.

Now and then I forced myself to use my camera, hoping that what I filmed might one day be used to set these animals free. The flood of emotions welling up in me became unbearable to the point where I just couldn't look at the animals any more. At the end of the pathway I noticed a long building with its windows blacked out. I peered through whatever openings I could find, hoping I might find the chimp inside, but the building appeared to be full of surplus equipment and furniture. If the chimp was at the zoo then someone had done a good job of hiding it for when I met up with Phillip and Mark I heard that they had found nothing either.

In the meantime it appeared that Alissa, the police captain and the manageress had become involved in a heated discussion. We didn't understand a word of what was being said but that didn't stop us from staring at them out of curiosity. I walked a short distance away and began to film the event. This was when Salim walked up to me. I thought to myself that if ever there was a stereotype of an Arab gangster it was Salim. His sunglasses, smart clothes and general demeanour pointed to a lifestyle that did not involve time in the office.

'This is bullshit … we must just take the bitch to the car and cut her fingers off,' he said calmly.

I chuckled, but when I looked up at him my smile disappeared. He was dead serious.

'I have bolt cutters in the back of my car,' he added.

I was shocked into silence and a few uncomfortable seconds passed as I digested his words and contemplated what an appropriate response might be. I knew this was a tough part of the world ... but actually cutting someone's fingers off to get information out of them ...? I could imagine the newspaper headlines: *Jane Goodall cuts fingers off.* Her name would certainly catch the attention of the world. I now had some idea of the sort of people I was becoming involved with.

'I don't think that will be necessary,' I said eventually. 'Not yet, anyway.'

He responded with a slight grin, never taking his eyes off me. It was as though he was trying to read my thoughts, to see whether or not I would play by his rules.

'Suit yourself. We'll talk again,' he said.

My attention returned to the shouting match that was now seriously out of hand. I returned to Phillip and Mark, hoping that between us we could come up with a more sensible approach. At the same time Alissa came towards us.

'The manageress is saying that the chimp is sick and has been taken to a veterinarian,' she said, clearly frustrated. 'The woman is refusing to tell us where the chimp is and the coward of a police officer doesn't want to arrest her!'

'The chimp is gone and they are not going to give it up,' Mark said in his usual flat tone.

'The officer is allowing her to make phone calls all the time,' Alissa added, shaking her head in disbelief.

The manageress was a very attractive Middle-Eastern woman and for the life of me I couldn't understand how someone with her looks and sophisticated manner could possibly work in a place like this. Letting her use the phone, however, was a critical mistake and this became apparent a short while later when a 'sharp' looking older man arrived. It's strange how lawyers all look the same and have the same attitude. He walked straight up to the police officer and started barking orders in Arabic. The officer stuttered, obviously intimidated.

'Shove the camera in his face!' Mark shouted. Realising that he had a point, I immediately switched the camera on and walked closer to them. When he saw what was happening, the lawyer shoved his open hand up against the lens and shouted at me in Arabic.

'No sprecanzi Arabic, man,' I told him cheekily, but he thought it wise to warn the police officer, who promptly told me in English to switch the camera off.

The lawyer insisted that he be given a few minutes to consult privately with his client and when he rejoined the captain he was more forthcoming about the whereabouts of the chimpanzee. However, it wasn't quite what we expected. He announced that the chimpanzee was ill and had been taken to a veterinarian for treatment and would have to remain there for some time under observation.

Alissa pounced on the opportunity to ask for the location of the veterinarian, but this was where the cooperation ended. The lawyer informed us that the confiscation order did not oblige his client to disclose the whereabouts of the animal; the order only allowed us to

Cozy (Francois Theron)

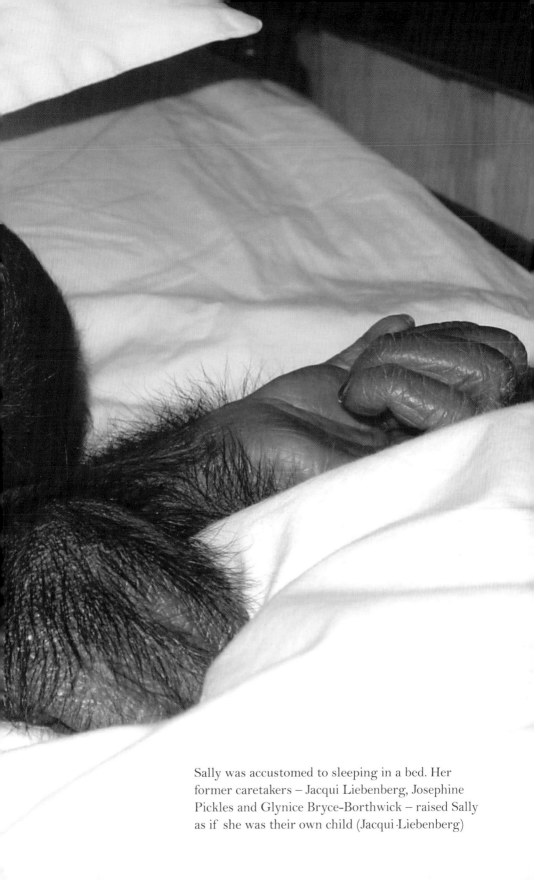

Sally was accustomed to sleeping in a bed. Her former caretakers – Jacqui Liebenberg, Josephine Pickles and Glynice Bryce-Borthwick – raised Sally as if she was their own child (Jacqui Liebenberg)

Azzi, Dinka, Nina and Thomas – the first chimps to be rescued from the Sudan. The picture was taken in the quarantine facility just after they had completed the compulsory three months' isolation (Francois Theron)

Zeena after her arrival at Chimp Eden from the United Arab Emirates. Her hair was cut and parts of her body were shaved by her previous owners (Eugene Cussons)

Zeena after being removed from her crate when
she arrived at Chimp Eden (Eugene Cussons)

Few chimps have as colourful a personality as Cozy. Here he
is seen enjoying the great outdoors (Francois Theron)

Picture taken of Charlie, the infant
chimp at the zoo in Beirut, only days
before he disappeared (Jason Mier)

Right: Sally at the age of one is more agile than
human baby of the same age. Here she explore.
her caretaker's work station (Jacqui Liebenberg

Zac was chained to the same tree for more than 17 years at a nightclub in Luanda (Lucinda Piets)

Eugene bonding with Marco in the Sudan (Triosphere Productions)

take possession of the chimp if it was on the premises of the zoo. That was where our legal rights ended. The captain's hands were tied. He couldn't make any arrests, or at least any arrests that wouldn't be immediately overturned by a good lawyer.

This was more than just a setback. Not only were we not going to get the chimp, but we had come up against a significant problem that we could possibly encounter when swooping on the other confiscation locations. If the owners were not criminally liable for illegally holding a CITES 1 endangered species, the confiscation order wouldn't be worth the paper it was written on because all the owners had to do was hide the chimps.

As incredible as it may sound, the owner was within his rights and the captain told us in his broken English that he couldn't do anything if the chimpanzee was not at the zoo. A different legal remedy would be required to handle this situation and it was one that he couldn't advise us on. He looked at Salim who was standing to one side, still cool and calm and seemingly unsurprised by the developments. He just grinned. He had known this would be the outcome. Surely these bastards were not going to be allowed to get away with it?

One has to accept that the law isn't perfect. If I had backed Salim we might already have the chimp. Maybe he knew what worked to get information out of people but I wasn't going to be persuaded to go down that path. As angry as I was, I knew we had to let it go. We had lost this round but maybe we could figure out a way to turn things around. I'm not the kind of person who accepts defeat easily. But this wasn't my mission and the back seat was where I belonged for now.

Mark was angry too, but he hid it well. Alissa and Monique did however take the time to voice their disappointment with the law, and the poor captain got a tongue lashing. We were leaving empty-handed but at least we had learned something about the law: we would only be successful in the confiscations if the animals were on site. If not, this failure would be repeated. There was no reason to believe that the other two locations would use the same legal argument but the only way for us to know for sure would be to get there as quickly as possible.

As we made our way back to the car, disappointed and tired, we vented our frustration in what can only be described as colourful language. That evening we would get together with all the members of the BETA team to lick our wounds and perhaps to strategise.

As we drove along the busy streets of Beirut that evening I noticed how the city had been transformed from a dusty concrete jungle into a dazzling fountain of lights; the city definitely looked more alive at night than during the day. Lebanon has a terrible history of conflict and the people are no strangers to an environment of danger and intimidation. A tragic civil war had plagued the country from 1975 to 1990 leaving ugly scars on the city buildings and, as I would find out, on the people themselves. It's difficult to imagine the effects that such a war can have on people, and especially difficult for people who have never lived through such an experience. Although South Africa had never descended into civil war, I had some idea of what this was like.

As a young boy I had lived through a time of farm attacks as South Africa struggled with itself. The majority of South Africans had been repressed under apartheid and their struggle for freedom resulted in an atmosphere of fear and violence. Neither side was innocent, but I was witness to a number of farm attacks and the unrest that took place in many rural areas and I had lost family members and neighbours in these sporadic assaults. I remember sitting in front of a closed window staring out into the brightly lit bush and trees surrounding the house anticipating an attack at any moment and knowing that if I did not have the courage to shoot first it could mean the difference between life and death. The world eagerly awaited the end of apartheid and, fortunately for all, it was followed by a positive transformation. It was, however, a struggle that affected all the people of South Africa, and the slow pace of transition has left many inequalities. Farm attacks persist to this day and rural landowners have had to develop a culture of awareness, readiness and response. I imagined it had been much worse for the people of Lebanon. The bullet-riddled buildings spoke for themselves.

I thought again about the situation in which I now found myself. We had spent a small fortune on building crates and logistical planning, and now it seemed there was a good possibility of my ego being bullet-riddled by returning home empty-handed.

We gathered at a Starbucks coffee franchise where the smell of freshly ground coffee helped to lift our spirits. The handful of BETA volunteers – all women in their late twenties and early thirties – were accustomed to putting on brave faces in times of hardship and we could not have wished for better company. We shared our views and discussed what we felt the police should have done, but this did not change the fact that we were no closer to achieving what we had set out to do. As I sat at the end of the long table listening to the conversation, I couldn't get rid of the feeling of despair that drifted over me. You didn't need to be a genius to know that if you missed your chance at taking the bad guys by surprise, you might never catch them at all. I had to believe that there was still a prospect of finding the chimpanzees. Even though I wasn't leading this mission, I somehow managed to convince myself that I was not going to give up. We simply had to keep trying ...

Mark stayed with Alissa that evening, while Monique was kind enough to take us in. She shared an apartment with her father, Mr Massih. Lebanese people have completely different lives to the one I was used to as a farm boy with wide open space around me and spacious single-storey houses. Here people seemed to be comfortable in apartment blocks and Monique was no different. Phillip and I shared a room – something that wasn't without its own challenge. There was only one access route to the two beds which meant one person had to get into bed first in order for the second to take possession of his. This definitely constituted 'uncharted territory' for both of us and I could tell from Phillip's reaction that he was a bit uncomfortable to find himself sleeping so close to another man! But Monique's hospitality meant we didn't have to spend money on hotel rooms. This was important as it brought down the costs of the mission giving us 'change' to channel into other challenges.

I would have thought that the day's activities, and especially the disappointing end to it, would have left me exhausted, but I had a restless night mulling over the various scenarios that might unfold the next day. Phillip, on the other hand, did not seem too fazed and was snoring away in no time at all. At some point I drifted off to sleep and was woken by the noise of the early morning traffic in the street below. Not wanting to waste any time, I got out of bed immediately and got ready to go. Phillip and Monique were just as eager to get moving.

Our first stop was for breakfast at a bakery a few blocks from the apartment. After that, the plan was to pick up Alissa and Mark and set off at once on the second confiscation attempt.

'Why a bakery for breakfast?' I asked Monique.

With a puzzled look on her face, she replied, 'What else?' Until then I had not thought about what a society of predominantly Muslim people had for breakfast in place of the western bacon-and-eggs.

'Sorry,' I said. 'I guess my brain isn't firing on all cylinders this early in the morning. I forgot for a moment that I'm in a Muslim country.'

The Jeep Cherokee pulled into an empty parking lot and the charming entrance to the bakery came into view. I was amazed to see a building that looked as though it had been designed in The Netherlands with a gigantic windmill looming over the entrance. It might not be serving bacon and eggs but I had the feeling that they were serving something good inside.

As we walked into the bakery the aroma of freshly baked bread was thick in the air. But as I studied the menu displayed above the beautiful clay oven my mind started racing again and I could feel a cold sweat engulfing me just thinking about the possibility of returning home without the chimps, the mission a complete failure. This early in my career I was not only inexperienced in working with chimps, I was also inexperienced at knowing myself.

Hiding my anxiety, I said to Monique: 'I guess you are going to be ordering for us.' Phillip was also looking confused by the unfamiliar menu. Monique ordered us a couple of manoush pastries which I was happy to discover tasted every bit as good as they looked. (A word of caution, though: the manoush might taste better than the English breakfast but it packs a heartburn punch of note.)

I took the liberty of ordering three coffees to go and once again this turned out to be exotic. The small cups resembling traditional espresso cups contained Turkish coffee which was so strong made my hair stand up. Trying not very successfully to hide my reaction to the powerful brew, I asked Monique: 'So, what is the plan for this morning?'

'We are going to pick up Alissa and Mark and then we are going to the second place where a chimpanzee is being held – a restaurant called Mr Steak.'

'I take it the police are going to meet us there?' Phillip asked.

Monique rolled her eyes. 'Yes, and hopefully that stupid captain will do a better job this time.'

Mark and Alissa were waiting for us at the entrance to Alissa's apartment block. I joined Phillip in the back of the vehicle so that Mark could sit in front. We didn't have to ask for news as Mark gave us an update as soon as we were on the road.

'We know the chimp is definitely not at the restaurant,' he said, 'but I'm hoping the police will force the guy to tell us where it's being kept.'

'That puts us in the same situation as yesterday,' I said. 'If the guy doesn't want to talk, what can we do about it?' It was a rhetorical question: if the owner wasn't intimidated by the police we were pretty well screwed.

'Well, I'm hoping the police will be able to force this guy to talk,' Mark answered in his usual flat tones. He has a lot of other animals and the confiscation order might scare him into talking.'

Although it seemed important to follow up each location as quickly as possible, we were in fact following the same pointless strategy as the day before, but there seemed to be no alternative. All we could do was hope that the owner scared easily.

'I don't understand how all these chimps can just disappear,' said Phillip. 'I mean, it's not that easy to move them and it's even less easy to keep them quiet.'

'What is the plan if we do manage to find out where the chimp is?' I asked.

'We go get a crate and go back to the chimp,' said Mark, 'and then you two take over – that is to say if the owner cooperates, but I'm not holding my breath.'

'Where is this place anyhow?' I was hoping to get some sense of where we were driving to.

'Sin-al-Fil, and we're here,' Monique said as she pulled the car over to the side of the road.

I looked out of the window expecting ·to see some structure that would provide evidence that an animal was being housed here, but there was none. It once again showed how exotic animals could be kept anywhere, in any facility, and that finding them without inside information was an impossible task. As far as we knew, the chimp could be anywhere in Lebanon.

'Do any of you see the police captain?' Alissa asked, scanning the area surrounding the restaurant. After a while we saw a number of police officers approaching the entrance to the restaurant. I switched my camera on and got out of the vehicle. As we approached them I noticed that the captain was chatting to his fellow officers. I wish I could say that they looked happy to see us, but most of them just looked annoyed at having to be there, probably expecting the same experience as the day before. Still, the captain at least greeted us cordially.

Alissa and Monique didn't waste any time before they began haranguing the captain. Once again it was in Arabic so the heated conversation was wasted on me, but one thing was clear: Alissa and Monique were doing most of the talking. I was pretty sure they were insisting that the captain should grow a spine!

'Maybe we should go and have a look inside,' Phillip said to Mark and me.

'I'll interrupt them and ask if we can go and take a peek,' I said and walked up to Alissa. 'Sorry to interrupt, but we were wondering if we could go inside and snoop around?'

I half expected the captain to yell at me for interrupting but he merely looked annoyed. 'No, don't worry, we are going in now,' he said and started to walk slowly towards the door, all the while staring at the confiscation order in his hand as if hoping it would miraculously change into something less challenging.

He walked through the entrance doorway with the other officers, Alissa and Monique close behind. Mark, Phillip and I were the last to enter the building. A large acrylic tank was visible immediately to the right of the doorway. The dirty water in the tank contained a solitary Nile crocodile. With scarcely any room to move around, this animal was clearly sentenced to a miserable existence. If this was an indication of what was to come, I was not looking forward to it.

The captain was talking to a waiter who simply nodded his head before walking through what seemed to be the entrance to the kitchen. A few minutes later the waiter returned accompanied by an overweight Arabic gentleman. The captain shook hands with the owner and then handed over the piece of paper without hesitation. The owner, a Mr Naifeh, took his time studying the document and his response, when it came, might have been the reason the captain had been so reluctant to enter the restaurant. He went absolutely berserk, shouting and waving his hands wildly.

Like lionesses pouncing on their prey, Alissa and Monique rushed in and started contradicting him. At this point the captain looked over his shoulder at his men and signalled to them to start searching. The men started off towards a small open air courtyard at the far end of the restaurant. We weren't going to stand around like statues and so we followed them immediately. Once in the courtyard the horrors of the place were revealed to us. The 200-yard courtyard was lined with cages on both sides. The animals and birds confined in them were calling frantically, beating on the mesh that held them captive. The smell of excrement was heavy in the air. I'd like to think they sensed their salvation was at hand but in truth I think the police and the rest of us all arriving at once had scared them witless. At the far end of the courtyard was a single cage and from what we could see it had only one occupant, a juvenile Hamadryas baboon.

As one, Mark, Phillip and I walked up to the cage. The young male baboon paced frenetically back and forth along the front of the cage, stopping every few seconds to extend his arm through the bars towards us, with an open cupped hand, as though asking for food.

'Be careful not to go too close, he might try and grab you,' Phillip warned as we slowly moved forward.

'The cage is filthy!' I blurted out in disgust on seeing excrement and piles of rubbish lying all over the inside of the cage. I manoeuvred closer to the cage and sat down on my haunches. That brought me to the same level as the young baboon. He stopped pacing for a moment, looked me straight in the eye and slowly extended his open hand towards me. Even though I felt desperately sorry for this wretched creature I knew that I couldn't take hold of his hand. Phillip had told me that abused animals often lure unsuspecting humans towards them so that they can unleash their pent-up anger or grab something that could be used as leverage to obtain food. This was the reason for Phillip's missing index finger. He had once taken care of an adult chimpanzee at the Johannesburg Zoo which had formerly been a circus chimp and for some reason he had grabbed hold of Phillip's hand at a time he least expected it.

I broke the moment by looking over my shoulder at the heated argument that seemed to be escalating out of control. The two women had no intention of letting the police captain handle this one on his own. Time was of the essence; if the owner's lawyer arrived on the scene the outcome would be inevitable. I went back inside to find out if the guy was giving up any information. As I approached, I could see that Monique was both angry and emotional.

'He says the chimp is dead.'

'Oh, come on!' I snapped. 'That's the oldest trick in the book. Does he think anyone here is stupid enough to believe him?'

'I know! That's what we've told him. We had someone come to this restaurant two days ago and the chimp was still here.'

'Where was the chimp being kept?' I asked.

'In the cage with the baboon,' she answered pointing to the cage I'd just left in the courtyard.

'So what is the captain trying to do?'

'He says he wants to see the corpse,' she said. 'Let's go and listen.'

Of course it was pointless for me to stand and listen as I couldn't understand a word of what was being said. But it started to look as though history was repeating itself. A few men wearing partially unbuttoned shirts walked in accompanied by a man in a nicely tailored suit. I muttered 'Oh boy, here we go again' to myself as my worst fears were confirmed; one of the new arrivals was Naifeh's lawyer and he immediately took charge. He insistently badgered the captain for a private conversation away from the two women who were as belligerent as ever.

Needless to say we were disgusted when the captain agreed to this and motioned us to step away. But worse was to come when, after a few minutes, the captain called Alissa and told her to bring everyone involved in the confiscation order to a table for further discussion.

I politely declined to sit down as I usually prefer to be on my feet with my back to the wall in a room full of snakes. Fortunately no one took offence at this. Phillip somehow managed to stay with the baboon without anyone objecting. The captain started speaking in Arabic, his gaze fixed on Alissa and Monique who were the only ones in our party who spoke Arabic. When they both looked up with shocked expressions on their faces Mark insisted on a translation. Alissa obliged and I leaned forward to hear what she had to say.

'What? This is bullshit!' Mark said, turning from Alissa to the captain and flinging his arms in the air. I snorted, shaking my head in disbelief.

The gist of the translation was as surprising as it was ridiculous. The captain was asking why BETA had acquired the confiscation order when the chimp had allegedly been dead for some time, and Naifeh was now making a counter-charge of harassment because, he alleged, he was the owner of a small, legal collection of animals. To me, it looked like the good captain had found it easier to take the side of the owner rather than challenging him and his lawyer.

The captain added another statement in Arabic, and Alissa translated. 'He wants you to hand over your passports.'

'I'm an American citizen!' Mark shouted, his face red with anger. 'I refuse to hand over my passport. You make sure he understands that!'

By this time Phillip had joined us. 'There is no way we are going to hand over our passports,' I whispered to him. 'Things are turning really nasty here.'

'I agree,' Phillip responded. 'It's best we get out of here while we can.'

Mark called out to us: 'I advise you not to hand anything over to them!'

I nodded my agreement and put my hand on Monique's shoulder. 'Let's get out of here while we can,' I said. 'We are going to lose this one.'

Mark stood up and gestured to Alissa and Monique. 'We are leaving,' he proclaimed.

The atmosphere didn't allow for any exchange of pleasantries but at least the captain allowed us to leave without repeating his demand for our passports. My morale was at an all-time low. I had come halfway round the world on what I hoped would be my first rescue mission and the effort was turning into a colossal failure. I was sure everyone else in the team was also feeling pretty low.

As we approached the car Alissa and Monique paused to discuss the situation. But I felt we needed to get out of there as quickly as possible.

'Let's just get out of here before they change their minds,' I said.

Monique got into the driver's seat with Mark in the front passenger seat. Phillip, Alissa and I got into the back and we drove off quickly.

During the next few minutes there was a loud venting of anger, cursing and name-calling, everyone talking at the same time. I forced myself to try to get everyone back on to the same page.

'Okay, let's calm down and talk about what happened there,' I said. 'Everything happened so quickly that I didn't quite get why the captain wanted our passports.'

Monique was the first to answer. 'The asshole was listening to Naifeh who maintained that there was a conspiracy against him and that we had no right to harass him with the confiscation order. The captain thought it in his best interests to shift the blame to us and then he carried on about what big trouble we'd be in if Naifeh laid a charge of harassment.'

'I shudder to think what might have happened if we'd had to leave an animal behind,' I said, cringing at the thought. 'Okay, we know the chimp isn't dead. I mean, he obviously wouldn't have killed the chimp simply because he'd heard we were coming to confiscate it. The logical thing for him to do was hide the chimp.'

'It's not that easy to hide a chimp,' Phillip said. 'Am I right that this chimp was about ten years old?'

'Yes, and he was always very sweet,' Alissa said. 'We used to come and spend time with him here and could play with him through the bars.'

'That still doesn't make it easy simply to move a chimp and keep it quiet so that your neighbours don't hear its vocalising,' Phillip continued.

'I don't think people would necessarily report seeing an exotic animal,' Mark said. 'There's no reason for them to think it's wrong to have one.'

'Even if we did manage to find out where the chimp is, we won't be able to take him, right?' I asked. 'I mean, you just saw Captain Coward in there.'

'Actually,' said Mark in his usual quiet voice, 'we have a CITES permit that says otherwise. Our name is given as the owner of the chimps and provision is made for you to take ownership of it as soon as the transit to South Africa is completed. You see, none of these owners applied for permits because the chimps were illegally purchased and they had no import permits to start off with. Technically speaking, if we had found a chimp at the restaurant, Naifeh would have had no option but to give it up. The police would have had to confiscate it.'

'We still have one more location, don't we?' I asked.

'Yes, but we sent someone there to check and the chimp had also gone,' Monique reminded us.

Mark had gone quiet. Then he said suddenly, 'They are gone, we're not going to find them.'

His comment surprised us all. I hadn't thought him a person who'd be easily defeated, but then I didn't know him very well at all.

'You are saying that there's nothing to be done?' I said, a hint of irritation in my voice.

'All the owners have somehow managed to hide their chimps, and I don't see how we are going to find them. The police sure as hell aren't going to help us.'

'I think we should arrange a meeting with the head of the ministry of environmental affairs,' Alissa said. 'They issued the warrant so perhaps they can advise us on what to do now.' She immediately busied herself with her mobile phone.

'Yes, I think that's our best option,' Monique agreed.

A few minutes later Alissa ended her call. 'Okay, I spoke to Mr Fadallah and he said that there is nothing more he can do, but if we got an arrest warrant from a judge the owners could be forced to show us where the chimps are – or provide evidence that they are dead, as in Naifeh's case. If they don't, they could face arrest.'

The drive to the ministry building seemed to take for ever. The lump was back in my throat and a feeling of desperation had set in. I'd never regarded myself as a quitter, but the situation did seem pretty hopeless. Even if we managed to get an arrest warrant from a judge, we would most likely run into the same problem with the police not having the stomach to follow through. Frustrated and angry, I started thinking that it might just come down to stealing the chimps from the owners. Would I be able to do that? I was fast losing faith in the 'right' way of doing things.

'Who exactly is Mr Fadallah?' I asked.

'He is at the ministry of environmental affairs,' Alissa replied. He gave me the name of a judge we could approach. I suggest that we split up – I'll focus on getting a meeting with the judge and the rest of you could try to find out where the chimps are. We've been told one is with a vet and maybe we could find out where Naifeh lives and do some snooping around there.'

Alissa spoke with renewed determination, but Mark didn't seem to share her optimism. Clearly he was not convinced that the judge would provide an answer.

'Don't forget the owner of the gas station chimp, we should check him out as well,' Phillip said.

'Yes,' said Monique, 'we must still go there. Mr Hamieh is the owner of Hamieh Gaz.'

'I know someone who will be able to get us personal information about the owners,' Alissa said.

'The veterinarian is also not a problem. I can find his practice.' Monique was not to be outdone by her friend.

'Whatever we do, we'll have to act quickly,' Mark informed us. 'I'm leaving for Kenya in two days' time.'

'You're leaving in two days?' I couldn't hide my irritation.

Mark turned to me and said: 'Well, I didn't think we were going to run into this amount of trouble. I have to get back to Kenya before my next trip to Iran. I've got another investigation going on, and it's not a trip I can postpone.'

I wasn't very happy about what I was hearing. We had come halfway across the world to assist in a rescue that Mark had arranged and now he was telling us he was quitting. I looked at Phillip who stared at me over the rim of his spectacles. At least I could count on him to see this mission through and I wasn't planning on leaving until all avenues had been exhausted. Mark's strategy hadn't worked and if he left we would probably have to start from scratch. Perhaps that wasn't a bad thing.

We dropped Alissa and Mark off at Alissa's apartment block. They were going to focus on getting the arrest warrant from the judge that would force the owners to give up the chimps, while Monique, Phillip and I concentrated on trying to find the veterinarian who was keeping the infant chimp from the zoo. While she was driving Monique made a few phone calls to her BETA colleagues and in no time at all they came back with a likely suspect. The only problem was that neither Phillip nor I blended in with the surroundings. In our khaki trousers and navy blue long-sleeved sanctuary uniform shirts we really did stick out like a couple of sore thumbs. We hadn't planned on doing any undercover work, but at least it would be something that we could control. We didn't have to depend on the police or on plans drawn up by someone else.

In many ways, I'm a control freak who doesn't like to take the back seat. With the way things were turning out, I was happier doing everything myself and taking the chance of failure rather than sitting around and relying on someone else.

Monique pulled up at a busy intersection. Across the street was a very ordinary looking one-storey building surrounded by six-foot-high walls. It looked more like a pet shop than a veterinary practice. Outside there were about eight small cages containing puppies stacked one on top of the other. A few exotic birds were also visible, including a South American macaw – yet another species that was a long way from home.

'What's the plan?' I asked.

'I'll go in and find out whether or not the vet is there,' Monique said. 'After that, I don't know.' She was also new to the role of private detective.

'Chimps are very noisy,' Phillip told her. 'So just nose around inside and maybe you'll hear chimp sounds.'

'If this young chimp is anything like Sally she'll be as noisy as hell,' I said. 'I can see that the building has an outside courtyard so I'm going to hang around there while you're inside. Maybe I'll hear something.'

We crossed the street together before going our separate ways. The sidewalk was crowded with pedestrians and I began to wonder whether I'd hear anything at all above the noise and the rumble of traffic. None the less, I leaned against the outer wall of the courtyard listening for any sound that resembled chimpanzee vocalisation. After ten minutes I had heard nothing other than the sort of faint sounds you would associate with domestic pet shop animals.

Eventually Monique came out of the building. She stopped on the sidewalk and looked in my direction. I immediately walked towards her, eager for information.

'I didn't hear anything, so I asked to speak to the vet,' she said.

'You did what?' I asked in amazement.

'He denied having the chimp and ushered me out of the door.'

'Of course he did,' I said. 'Dr Evil isn't known for his honesty. This is a dead end – if we don't have a search warrant there's no way we can find out if he has the chimp.'

'I wish you good luck trying to get that from the cops,' she retorted.

Just then Monique's phone rang. It was Alissa. 'They've got a great lead from one of Alissa's connections,' she said, 'and would like to meet us at a coffee shop. We have to hurry.' She walked rapidly towards the car.

The three of us made our way across town to a small Arabic coffee shop where we found Mark and Alissa waiting outside.

'Who's the guy we're meeting?' I asked them.

'He called me out of the blue,' Alissa said, 'and I have no idea where he got my number or how he knows what we are doing. He wouldn't give me his name, just said he wanted to talk.'

'Maybe he'll be overwhelmed if we all go in,' I said. 'So who's it going to be?'

'I'll go with Alissa,' Mark volunteered.

'I'll go as well,' I said, 'since you won't be with us in two days' time.'

Phillip and Monique said they'd enjoy a cup of coffee while we tried to locate the mystery man.

'Obviously I don't know what he looks like,' Alissa said, 'but he said he would make contact with us.'

We scanned the interior of the restaurant. Most of the tables were taken, but at the far end of the room an older man was sitting at a table by himself. I guessed he was in his early fifties, slightly overweight and of Middle-Eastern descent. Neither of us wanted to embarrass ourselves by approaching the wrong person so we hovered near the entrance waiting for him to make the first move. I kept looking in his direction hoping to make eye contact and perhaps getting him to signal that he was the man we were meeting.

Suddenly a man started talking to Alissa. He was standing on her left and he spoke to her in Arabic and then motioned for her to lead the way to an empty table. We had been so preoccupied with looking for someone already in the room that we had failed to notice him approaching us from behind. This cloak-and-dagger business made me feel a bit uneasy. There was only one vacant table but it seemed to suit him fine. He sat down with his back to the wall and scrutinised both Mark and me before saying something to Alissa in Arabic.

I thought it would be a good idea to introduce myself. 'I'm Eugene,' I said, smiling and holding out my hand.

He hesitated for a second and then he took my hand. 'Salam,' he replied, the Arabic greeting which means 'peace'.

Annoyingly, the conversation was once again in Arabic. He spoke without interruption from Alissa and all Mark and I could do was look on and try not to feel like complete idiots. After a few minutes he gave Alissa the opportunity to ask a few questions, perhaps things she was unclear about. Then he got up from his chair, lifted his hand in farewell, and left.

Nothing was said until he had left the coffee shop.

'What did he have to say?' I asked impatiently.

'I'm in shock,' Alissa said, covering her mouth with her hand. 'He said he used to work for Mossad, but he didn't elaborate on that. The problem apparently goes much deeper than chimps being sold at pet shops. It seems there is a single kingpin smuggler who supplies all the pet shops from which people can order a chimp.'

The best was still to come. 'He said that it was the airport veterinary clerk who warned the smuggler about the pending confiscation. The smuggler, a man called Hajjar, contacted all chimp owners so that he could take the chimps into hiding until the confiscation efforts were abandoned.'

This was indeed a revelation. Not only did we now understand how the trade in endangered animals worked in Lebanon, but we also knew why the chimps all disappeared around the same time. The information would enable us to draw up an effective strategy to find the chimps. We now knew that it was a single person who controlled the supply of chimps and simple logic would imply that all the chimps would be kept at one location controlled by that person.

Alissa added: 'He mentioned that the smuggler was also suspected of dealing in drugs, so these are not the sort of people we want to mess with.'

'Wow, all this information from one guy!' I said rather sarcastically. 'Who is he? James Bond?'

'I don't see why he would lie to us,' Mark said. 'What could he possibly gain by giving us false information?'

'On the other hand, I don't see why Mossad would be interested in this smuggler unless there was some connection to Israel, which I doubt,' I said, adding another sceptical opinion to the mix. Officially known as the Institute for Intelligence and Special Operations, Mossad was an

Israeli organisation primarily tasked with intelligence gathering and covert operations both in and outside Israel.

'*Ex*-Mossad,' said Alissa, 'and he wouldn't say how he had come by this information.'

'I still don't think he has any reason to lie to us,' Mark said.

'Okay,' I replied. 'Let's say that we believe him. What's our next move?'

'I still think it is sensible to focus on getting the arrest warrant from the judge,' said Alissa.

'If that fails we'll be screwed,' I said. 'I think we need a back-up plan.'

'We still have to go to the owners' houses. I got all the addresses while you guys were at the vet.'

'Damn, you work fast, Alissa!'

Phillip and Monique joined us and we gave them an update on the meeting with Mr Ex-Mossad. For the most part, we were in agreement about the sincerity of the mysterious informant, but none of us were quite sure what to do with the information. There were gaps in our intelligence. We had a name but no knowledge of where he lived or worked. Phillip pointed out that it would be too cumbersome for Hajjar to hide the chimps at different locations because of the physical problems associated with caretaking, not to mention the noise levels. Alissa then mentioned that with the help of some people she knew we might be able to fill in the missing information.

We were all starting to feel excited. We didn't have a definite plan yet, but we now knew who was behind the disappearance of the chimps and that at least was a start. So far, Hajjar had outsmarted us but we now had a chance of turning things in our favour. Alissa and Mark confirmed that they would follow up on obtaining the warrant from the judge, giving the rest of us time to look into other leads. It was already late in the afternoon, so we decided to use the remaining hours of daylight to visit the residential addresses Alissa had obtained for Naifeh and Hamieh. If we found any signs of the chimps at the addresses it would mean that Mr Ex-Mossad had lied to us and was deliberately misleading us for reasons we couldn't possibly guess at.

As the last rays of afternoon sun lit up the hills of Beirut the Jeep made its way up the winding roads that connected the suburbs. Small apartment blocks littered the landscape. I had no idea how Monique managed to find her way to our destination, which was little more than a street address; to me all the neighbourhoods looked similar. As we rounded yet another bend in the road the vehicle slowed down and the conversation in Arabic between Alissa and Monique picked up as they pointed out a faded pink, four-storey apartment block slightly below the elevation of the road. Monique parked the car on the side of the road and announced that she had found Hamieh's home.

'Which apartment does he own?' I asked studying the building through the side window.

'All of them,' Alissa answered. 'Some Lebanese families choose to live together in the same building, if they can afford it.'

I found it hard to believe that an entire extended family, including the in-laws, would get along well enough to live together, but then again this wasn't a part of the world I was familiar with.

From our vantage point we could see almost all the open areas of the building. If Hamieh was hiding the chimp at his house, he wouldn't be so foolish as to make the chimp visible to the passing public. Mark and I got out of the car and walked down the street trying not to make it obvious that we were surveying the building. Down the street I noticed what looked like a Christian church which people appeared to be exiting before going their separate ways. I suddenly felt exposed. I was so obviously a foreigner and I was walking down a street that contained no significant tourist attraction. I really needed to sort out my cover if I was going in for this cloak-and-dagger stuff.

I stopped and stared sheepishly into the middle distance as people walked past me. Almost all of them looked at me as if I did not belong. This didn't seem to bother Mark who strode ahead and eventually found a way of walking around the apartment building. I opted to listen instead for chimp vocalisations. Chimpanzees in general are noisy animals. They have very loud vocalisations and, from what I'd been told, became particularly vociferous if confined in an area where there was a lot of activity going on around them in terms of the movement of people and other distractions.

I listened for fifteen minutes but heard nothing. If there was a chimp inside the building it was keeping dead quiet. My mind started to wander and my imagination took over. If the chimp was being kept inside, where was it? I imagined a dark cellar, with the owner visiting only once or twice a day to bring it food. The truth was, I had no proof of anything and the police were certainly not going to entertain my fanciful notions of animal abuse.

As I walked back to the car I met Mark who by now had circumnavigated the building. As usual, his face showed no emotion.

'I walked around but there's nothing,' he said.

'I heard nothing either.'

'This isn't going to work,' he added. 'The only way to be sure is to get the police to go inside.'

'I think Naifeh is going to be exactly the same,' I said with a sigh. 'None of these guys are dumb enough to leave the animals in plain sight.'

Disappointed, we returned to the Jeep, leaving immediately for Hamieh Gaz Station. We already knew that the chimp was not at the station, but that didn't stop us from hoping that it might be back in its cage. It was 8pm by the time we reached the station and there was nobody to be seen. The cage, which was located a mere 20 yards from the fuel pumps, was empty. The chimp that it had once housed had vanished without a trace. We rolled down the windows and listened. This part of Beirut seemed to slow down at night; there was no sound of vehicles or people, just a deathly silence. We remained parked at the side of the road for about half an hour, analysing every sound that might provide a clue to the presence of the chimp. But there was none.

Shaking my head, I rolled up the window. 'I guess our informant was right ... for now.' The feeling of disappointment in the car was tangible.

'We'll start with the judge first thing in the morning,' Alissa said.

We dropped Mark and Alissa off and returned to Monique's apartment where her father was waiting for us as we walked through the door. He greeted his daughter warmly.

I held out my hand. 'I'm Eugene.'

'Of course you are,' he replied with a smile on his face.

I hesitated for a few seconds and then burst out laughing. I had been caught off guard, but the change in mood was refreshing.

'What are you guys doing here looking for monkeys?' he asked with a grin. 'This is Lebanon, not Africa.'

'Well, I heard you had plenty of them here,' I said with a chuckle.

'Let's go look for some,' he answered and ushered us towards the door.

'He is going to take us out for dinner,' Monique said.

Mr Massih was in good shape for a man who looked to be in his early sixties. I liked him immediately; he was friendly and did not seem to mind our dragging his daughter around Beirut in search of smuggled animals. When we got to the car he told me to sit in front. I suspected he wanted to know more about why we were in Beirut. As we drove towards downtown Beirut, Mr Massih's positive vibe began to rub off on all of us. While Phillip and Monique were chatting in the back I struck up a conversation with the man.

'We are having a hard time finding the chimps,' I told him.

'You are not going to find them,' he said flatly.

'What makes you say that?' I asked, surprised. I wasn't sure if he was joking again.

'The people you are dealing with are tough and won't show you any kindness for what you are doing.'

'Hey, I'm tough as well,' I said jokingly.

He didn't reply but the look on his face was cynical.

A bullet-riddled building came into view. The damage was severe and I could only imagine the intensity of the fire fight that had caused it.

I whistled. 'That must have been a damned hard fight.'

'You have no idea. I was a commander during the civil war and I fought in these streets.'

This didn't surprise me; he had the demeanour of a military man. As we drove on we passed a high-rise building that looked as though it was still under construction.

'That used to be the Hilton Hotel. Do you see the tank in front of it?' He pointed to the rusty mangled remains of an armoured vehicle.

'Yes, it looks as though it's been blown to pieces.' I looked past him at the wreckage.

'I blew it up with an RPG,' he said proudly.

A rocket propelled grenade is an anti-tank weapon launched from the shoulder. It wasn't every day you got to meet a man who had been so closely involved in a devastating conflict and lived to tell the tale.

'Do you prefer 7.62 or 5.56?' I asked. Having grown up in a military household, I knew something about guns and thought it might be a topic of mutual interest.

He casually lifted the front of his shirt while keeping one hand on the steering wheel, revealing scarring that looked like gunshot entry wounds.

'You could say I prefer 7.62 as it's kind of part of myself,' he said with a grin.

The civil war raged for fifteen years. It was a conflict that ravaged the country and here, sitting beside me, was a man who had been in the thick of it, fighting for what he believed in. The AK-47 with its 7.62 cartridge has found its way into almost every corner of the world, notably into the hands of guerrilla fighters and terrorists. Its ease of use, low maintenance and large projectile make it ideal for the military and almost every African country arms its soldiers with the weapon. With conflict zones and liberation wars starting and ending on a regular basis in Africa, soldiers who find themselves without a war to fight often end up using this weapon to poach the very species of animal I had come to Beirut to rescue. It is estimated that there are between fifty and seventy million AK-47s spread throughout the world, so it is not difficult to believe that they are easily accessible to poachers. In comparison, the 5.56 projectile fired from the American-made M16 assault rifle was less common in this part of the world, its high cost and high maintenance being unattractive to liberation fighters.

'I was running down the stairs of the Hilton Hotel during heavy fighting,' said Monique's father, 'when I ran into a soldier from the opposition coming towards me. I saw him first and emptied my M16 clip into him, but it wasn't enough to stop him from getting off a shot or two … the 5.56 does not pack enough punch.'

I didn't quite know how to respond, so I simply raised my eyebrows.

The dinner was a unique experience for me as it was the first time I had eaten a traditional Middle-Eastern mezze with hummus and various smaller dishes. It turned out that Mr Massih and I had many more things in common and the four of us enjoyed a memorable evening.

FOUR
POINT OF NO RETURN

In spite of enjoying a great dinner and evening out, I was restless again and tossed and turned all night long. Eventually the sun's orange rays were dancing on the wall opposite the window and I decided I would be better off taking a walk than wallowing in negative thoughts. Of course, the root of my restlessness had to do with the fact that we were no closer to getting the chimpanzees than the day we arrived in Beirut. The first few days found us chasing our tails, but a bizarre turn of events provided us with crucial information that might just put us ahead of the game. But what we were actually going to do had to be carefully thought through and planned.

Earlier, I had noticed a small bakery down the street from the apartment and this seemed to be a good destination for my early morning walk. The crisp morning air was quite unlike the air at home and I was starting to miss my home and everything that made it special, especially my wife Natasha. I had barely spoken to her the last couple of days fearing that I would have to disclose that I'd come here for nothing or, worse, having to tell her what I was getting myself into. But Natasha has this incredible calmness about her, something I really admired. This wasn't the first time we had been apart. I used to take clients on exploration safaris all over southern Africa. Perhaps it was those trips that made her confident that I would always find my way home. But I felt it would serve no purpose at this point to distress her or anyone else back home.

The streets were quiet. An elderly gentleman was sweeping the pavement in front of his fresh produce store. He looked up at me for a moment, probably wondering what the hell a foreigner was doing walking the streets so early in the morning. The inside of the bakery was brightly lit and I got a homely feeling as I walked through the doorway. Friendly smiles greeted me as I walked up to the display cases and for a moment I almost forgot my problems and the fact that my job seemed to focus more on negative issues than positive ones. I could not decide which of the delightful looking delicacies to choose and this simple feeling of indecision was curiously uplifting. In the end I selected some of the small round pastry balls called 'awwamaat' and they were every bit as delicious as they looked.

The traffic was building up as I walked back to the apartment; people were starting their day and it was time that we got busy too. Before we arrived in Beirut Mark had told me that one could buy a chimp from almost any pet shop. In a moment of clarity it occurred to me that the right strategy might be to pose as a buyer. Surely this would bring us closer to Hajjar? Waiting for the arrest warrant from the judge and placing our hope in the willingness of the police to cooperate didn't seem viable as the only strategy.

Monique and Phillip greeted me as I walked into the apartment.

'Where did you disappear to?' Phillip asked.

'I had to get some fresh air – and I think I have also come up with an idea that might work.'

'Let's hear it.'

'I think we should pose as buyers and hit the pet shops until we get lucky,' I said. 'Hajjar most likely doesn't know that we know about him and his tactics of hiding the chimps. If we can catch out one pet shop owner in the act of selling a chimp then if some pressure is applied they might be persuaded to squeal on the supplier.'

'I like it,' Phillip said. 'When do we start?'

'How about we grab a manoush at the bakery and then get started straight afterwards?'

'Sounds good,' said Monique, 'but I suggest we start at a pet shop that is not located in Beirut. There's a better chance that the shops further away will not have heard about us. And I'll also phone Alissa to make sure she and Mark handle the warrant of arrest while we pursue pet shop owners.'

We got in the Jeep and drove to Tripoli, the second largest city in Lebanon. The most interesting aspect of the drive up the coast was that one couldn't tell where Beirut started or ended – the fifty-mile journey was a succession of apartment blocks, one after the other. On the way Monique told us that not much was known about the shop we were targeting, apart from the fact that exotic animals had been spotted there by BETA volunteers. So we could not be certain we'd find a chimpanzee there.

With a population of more than 500 000 Tripoli was by no means small. The city had one of the largest seaports in the country and no doubt had the potential of being a Mecca for smugglers. But with so little information about how Hajjar operated, and so little time at our disposal, our task was not going to be an easy one. Our first stop was a pet shop in the centre of the city. It was a featureless building with not much about it to indicate what its trade was.

'We need a plan before we go in,' I said. 'We can't just march in and say we want to buy a chimp.'

I launched into my plan. 'I will act as a buyer for a private zoo in England. Phil, I need you to stay in the car and act like the boss man who is too important to get out of the car but has to okay any deals I make. So when I point you out don't wave at me all friendly-like – if anything, scowl at me.'

'Shouldn't be too difficult,' Phillip chuckled. 'How's your poker face?'

'Not as good as Mark's. Monique, you'll be my translator – someone I've hired to take me to all the places that might sell exotic animals.'

'Got it,' said Monique. 'Actually it's not far from the truth since neither of you understands a word of Arabic.'

Before we got out of the car I rummaged in my camera bag and rolled all the mission cash into a fat wad with a hundred-dollar bill visible on the outside. Then I put on my dark glasses and joined Monique who was waiting on the kerb. Trying to calm her nerves, she was hurriedly smoking a cigarette.

'Give me one, will you?' I asked her.

'But you don't smoke,' she said, a puzzled expression on her face.

'I do now,' I replied. 'It's part of the arrogant smuggler I'm about to become.'

My lungs objected to the cigarette the moment I lit it, but it was better I had my coughing fit outside and not in the shop.

'All right,' I said, 'let's get this over with before I lose my nerve.'

We crossed the road to the shop. The smell of dirty cages assailed me as I walked through the door, but I supposed that wasn't unexpected in a pet shop. There were several small mesh cages containing dogs and cats of all ages and we could hear birdcalls although we couldn't see any birds. But no exotic animals anywhere.

I walked up to the counter with Monique at my side and addressed the first man who turned his attention to us.

'Hi, my name is Burt, Burt Hamilton,' I said and extended my hand towards him.

'Salam,' the man replied.

'You speak English?'

'Yes.'

'Good man,' I said condescendingly. 'I work for a private zoo in England and I am interested in buying exotic animals.' I puffed on my cigarette, taking care not to inhale.

'What exactly are you looking for?'

'I want young chimpanzees,' I said, adding flippantly, 'you know, the monkey without the tail.'

'Wait a minute,' he said and went off to talk to a colleague standing a short distance away.

After a few moments, they both came back to us, the colleague talking in Arabic. Monique responded and a short conversation ensued. I took out the roll of cash and fiddled with the notes. Both men stared at it.

The first man turned and reached for a phone under the counter.

'He says he knows a guy who can help you,' Monique whispered to me.

'Let's hope he's not phoning Hajjar,' I whispered back, fighting the urge to cough. 'The game will be up if he is because Hajjar will tell him who we are.'

After a short discussion the colleague scribbled something on a piece of paper and handed it to Monique, explaining loudly with wild gesturing of his hands. I might have been imagining it but it seemed to me that he was a lot less polite when talking to Monique than to me.

'Okay, let's go,' she said, walking towards the door.

'What was that all about?' I asked. 'Do you think he's suspicious?'

'No, not at all,' Monique replied with a hint of annoyance in her voice. It's because I'm not wearing a veil. They are Muslim and detest women like me.'

'So, do we go to the address he gave you?'

'Yes, we can go.'

On the way to the car a taxi caught my eye. It was a 1980s model Mercedes Benz with a yellow TAXI sign on the roof. 'Would it be better to go in a taxi?' I asked.

'Yes, good idea.'

I gave Phillip a quick update as we walked to the taxi. With instructions from Monique the driver drove terrifyingly fast through narrow streets in which there was a large military presence. Armed soldiers patrolled the streets, some of which had been cordoned off by armoured personnel carriers. Evidently these were precautions in response to some sort of threat that we were not aware of. I knew very little about Middle-Eastern politics or the different organisations and tensions in the region. I had never heard of Hezbollah before I arrived in Beirut. The only organisation I knew anything about was Al Qaeda, and that was only because of the attack on the Twin Towers in New York.

'What's up with all the military in the streets?' I asked.

'There have been assassination threats on government officials and I think the Lebanese army is trying to maintain control. They regularly set up roadblocks to search vehicles for weapons and explosives.' She was nonchalant, as though describing just another day at the office.

'Well, I guess it's my luck to show up when things are ready to blow,' I said.

'Salim says everything is cool, so you don't have to worry.'

'What has Salim got to do with it?'

'Oh, he is part of Hezbollah,' she informed me. 'I think he's under the top militia men.'

'Hezbollah? Why does that sound familiar?'

'You probably hear in western news that Hezbollah are terrorists.'

'Let me get this straight: we've been hanging out with a big-shot terrorist and you don't think it's worth mentioning?'

'They are not considered terrorists here,' Monique said evenly. 'They are a political party that is part of the government. But nobody messes with them. They are allowed to carry any weapons they want to, do whatever they want. Salim just happens to be sympathetic to BETA and only wants to help us.'

She proceeded to give me further information about Hezbollah. Only after I'd left did I learn that the organisation first arrived on the scene in 1985 when Israel attacked Lebanon in response to the attempted assassination of the Israeli ambassador to the United Kingdom by a 'terrorist' group called the Nidal Organisation. Hezbollah were trained in Iran and were inspired by the controversial Ayatollah Khomeini, former spiritual leader of Iran.

The last thing I had expected when I embarked on this chimp rescue mission was getting involved with what to my mind was a terrorist organisation. There again, from Monique's perspective they could be considered freedom fighters – 'one man's terrorist is another man's freedom fighter'. No matter how sympathetic Salim was, if he was willing to take lives to further his cause that was something I could not condone.

The driver slowed down as the roads deteriorated. In the area which we were travelling through it was easy to see the transition from the homes of the wealthy to those of people living below the bread line. Even though it was winter, the temperature soared in the middle of the day. I rolled down the window hoping for some fresh air but was immediately met hit by a rush of hot air.

The driver turned right and said something in Arabic to Monique.

'He says the pet shop should be halfway up the hill.'

The pet shop came into view. On the pavement outside I could see a light-brown animal in a wire cage. My heart skipped a beat when I realised it was a primate of some sort. As we came closer my suspicions were confirmed. The adult male Hamadryas baboon, about three feet tall, was being kept in a cage no larger than a bathtub. This baboon species is native to northeast Africa and the Arabian Peninsula. They are particularly well adapted to higher altitudes and desolate areas where large predators seldom venture.

I asked the driver to stop the taxi a short distance away from the baboon so as not to excite or alarm it. The anger I felt at the sight of the animal being kept in such a tiny cage was almost blinding. I had visions of myself getting out of the car and forcing the pet shop owner into the cage after setting the baboon free. I had to restrain myself, to bury my feelings; my instinctive reaction would not bring us any closer to finding the chimpanzees. Anticipating some sort of interaction from us, the baboon grabbed the wire and shook the cage. Not receiving the desired response he dejectedly fell back on to his bum.

We were all shocked at the way in which the baboon was being treated, but there was little we could do about it. The law in Lebanon seemed to have no problem with the barbaric treatment of animals. I took a deep breath and got out of the taxi. There was no point in starting a conversation about the baboon. We were all profoundly upset but talking wasn't going to change anything. Of one thing I was convinced: we had found the right place to buy exotic animals and I was going to have to give the performance of my life if I was to convince the pet shop owner that I was sincere about wanting to buy a chimpanzee.

I waited on the pavement for Monique. 'Are you ready?'

'I have a terrible lump in my throat,' she said, visibly upset.

'Well, swallow it, will you?' I said unsympathetically while studying her face to see if she was going to cope. 'We have to sell this guy our story.'

Above the entrance to the shop was a sign that read TARZAN. How ironic, I thought. The Tarzan of fiction was raised by apes, depending on them for his survival and eventually becoming their leader, yet here was the exact opposite: the caging and enslavement of apes for the entertainment of humans.

The owner was standing in the centre of his shop busy putting out food for hordes of puppies that he had crammed into small mesh cages. I greeted the man first and then gave Monique the opportunity to do the same.

She briefly explained in Arabic that we had been referred to him and what our requirements were. Uncomfortable silences aren't good for business so I assumed my best British accent and started my charade: 'Burt Hamilton … I work for a wealthy animal trader in England who owns an exquisite private zoo. I'm looking to pay cash for a chimpanzee.'

Monique translated and he was quick to answer, looking me straight in the eye. Meantime, I took the roll of cash out of my pocket, removed the rubber band around it and folded it flat, as if about to start counting it out. Mesmerised by the sight of the cash, he answered Monique without taking his eyes off it.

'He says we must pay in advance,' she translated, 'and he will get us one within three hours.'

I refolded the notes and shoved them into my pocket. 'Not a chance. I'm only interested in animals that are in tip-top condition and if my boss doesn't like it, then there's no deal.' I grabbed the man by the arm and led him to the entrance to the shop.

'You see, he is waiting there and he is getting impatient.'

Monique translated and Phillip gave us his over-the-top-of-his-glasses stare before turning back to his magazine. The owner looked at Phillip and took the bait, hook, line and sinker. He began to give Monique details, counting off each item on the fingers of one hand.

'He says he can get us a ten-year-old chimp, a three-year-old chimp, and one that is around five years old. The prices start at $20 000 for the youngest one; the oldest one is a bit difficult and the price for him is only $5 000.'

It was starting to look as if we'd hit the jackpot. But there was no way I was going to hand over the mission funds simply in the expectation of seeing a chimp. I needed to get the owner, the chimps and the police in the same room – selling any great ape is illegal.

'I'm not going to pay unless I see the animal and can take a picture of it that I can show my boss,' I said, opening my camera bag and pointing inside. Monique translated.

The owner nodded. He mumbled something to Monique and walked towards a phone near the entrance.

'Will you listen in on his conversation?' I asked Monique. 'Maybe we'll learn something about where the chimps are being kept.'

Monique and I walked towards the entrance and I walked over to the baboon. Unfortunately, we had no legal reason for confiscating the animal. The baboon shuffled frantically in the cage when he saw me approaching, so I backtracked and knelt down so that I was at his level. A black Mazda sedan drove up the road and stopped next to the cage. It wasn't surprising that people would be drawn to investigate what was in the cage but what followed next appalled me. A veiled woman and a man I assumed to be her husband got out of the car with their two excited children. Clearly amused by the baboon, the children shouted and pointed excitedly. The man began to kick the cage to get a reaction out of the baboon who did not disappoint them with his angry warning call. The family exploded into loud laughter. He continued kicking the cage until his wife started getting irritated and they returned to their car and drove away.

I walked to the cage and began to talk to the baboon in a calm, quiet voice.

'It's okay, boy. Calm down.' I knew the words didn't matter; it was the tone of voice that the baboon would respond to. I took an apple from my bag and cut off slices with my penknife which I tossed into the cage. I felt a mixture of disgust and disappointment. Disgust at the man setting such a bad example to his children, and disappointment at myself for not doing anything to stop him. The owner of the shop was still talking on the phone and he would surely have become suspicious if I had intervened.

I walked back to Monique who was also upset by the behaviour of the family in the black car. One incident of this nature was perhaps not too surprising but what happened immediately afterwards really shook my faith in humanity. Another vehicle pulled up alongside the cage; two adults and a child disembarked and proceeded to do exactly the same thing – kicking the cage and laughing at the baboon's inevitable reaction. I desperately wanted to understand their behaviour but

I simply couldn't. It was totally beyond my comprehension. I was witnessing the evil cycle that ultimately results in the extinction of animals in conflict zones. War and instability over generations had resulted in people being taught that animals were not important. I felt numb, torn between what I regarded as my duty to protect animals and not wanting to jeopardise our chimp rescue mission.

I turned to face the owner who had now finished his phone call. He strode towards us, shouting at Monique in Arabic and gesticulating wildly. I stood firm. If he wanted to make trouble now seemed like a good time for me. Monique stepped behind me and the owner, realising I was not backing off, stopped, his face inches away from mine. I was expecting him to throw at least one punch but, disappointingly, he didn't.

'Let's go,' Monique muttered. 'Our plan hasn't worked.'

We turned away and walked back to the vehicle. The taxi driver was clearly intrigued and was trying to follow what was going on but I urged him to get going as quickly as possible.

'Anyone care to tell me what happened back there?' Phillip asked as the vehicle took off.

'I think he was talking to Hajjar,' Monique said.

'Ek sal jou alles vertel sodra ons by die kar kom,' I said in my home language of Afrikaans so that he understood I'd update him soon enough.

Phillip answered, 'Reg so', which meant he understood that I didn't want to talk in front of the taxi driver. He indicated to Monique that she should also remain silent.

Back at the Jeep we paid our taxi driver and started the three-hour journey back to Beirut. I updated Phillip on the turn of events; we were all in agreement that the pet shop owner was definitely sourcing his animals direct from Hajjar.

'We might have lost this round,' I said, 'but I think that Hajjar has shown his hand. We now know that the animals are within a three-hour journey of the pet shop and that they are all being held at one location, as we suspected. We also know that Hajjar controls all enquiries – that's why the owner got so upset when he realised that we weren't who we said we were.'

'What do we do now?' Monique asked.

'I think we should try one or two other pet shops in Beirut,' said Phillip. 'If we keep on insisting that we want to see the chimps before we buy one, we may be able to narrow down the location where they are being kept.'

Hajjar might still be one step ahead of us, but we were catching up. As we drove back to Beirut the experience with the Hamadryas baboon haunted me. My dilemma was that I knew I had to deal with callous individuals who viewed animals as useful only if they were a means to profit, but I didn't want to face the fact that Lebanese society was so uncaring that parents were teaching their children to abuse animals. And yet there were people like Alissa and Monique who took huge risks to protect animals, and the BETA shelter took care of hundreds of abandoned dogs and cats. The experience nevertheless had a profound impact on me – call it a loss of innocence. No longer would I be naive enough to believe that humans were inherently good. Could those who cared nothing for the welfare of animals be rehabilitated? Could we yet save the fauna and flora of the world? More importantly, while one could probably teach a person about the importance of nature, could you teach that person to *feel*?

The next five days raced past but the judge to whom we had applied for a warrant for the arrest of the chimp owners was dragging his feet. Mark left for Kenya, but the rest of us were willing to see the mission through to the very end, whenever that might be. We visited several more pet shops, all offering the same chimps at the same prices but everything went pear-shaped as soon as phone calls were made to Hajjar. It was incredibly frustrating to know the chimps were being kept somewhere close. Alissa identified several large properties registered in the name of Hajjar in the neighbourhoods of Shiyah and Ouzaii, but they were either deserted or too well secured to try to access them without taking enormous risks.

We had come to a dead end.

FIVE

JUDGEMENT DAY

On our ninth day in Lebanon it seemed that justice would be done. Although the judge had not produced any warrant, Alissa finally succeeded in obtaining an arrest warrant from the general prosecutor. With this in our hands we made our way to the police station to have it enforced.

The strong military presence we had witnessed in Tripoli a few days earlier had now spread to the capital and armoured personnel carriers and soldiers were out in force. The high court building and its immediate surroundings seemed to be an area of high priority for the military, although why this should be so was not clear to us.

The main street in front of the court, the adjacent ministry of justice building and the police station conducting the operation had all been cordoned off. We were advised to drive around the block and enter at the opposite end of the street. We did this, but Monique, not being absolutely sure where the street entrance was, pulled over to the side of the road and called out to a soldier for confirmation. The soldier, a young man armed with an M16 rifle, leaned in at the window to talk to Monique. He did not waste the opportunity of flirting with the two ladies sitting in the front of the car.

'We are wanting to get to the ministry of justice,' she said. 'Should we go up this next street?'

'Are you the people here to chase monkeys?' the soldier asked with a big grin on his face. We were dumbfounded. How was it possible that an ordinary infantryman knew what we were doing? I smelt the proverbial rat. Something was wrong and I got the distinct feeling we were driving into a trap. The soldier burst out laughing when Monique answered his question. He turned around and shouted something to his fellow soldiers and they too roared with laughter.

'You can drive up here,' he said. 'The building you are looking for is on the right.' He had hardly finished his sentence before he was once more overcome with laughter.

Monique parked in a small parking lot directly opposite the courthouse and we made our way to the ministry of justice. The streets were lined with soldiers and at the entrance to the building more soldiers were searching bags and briefcases as well as scanning with metal detectors for concealed weapons.

'I will go in to see the prosecutor,' Alissa said. 'He asked that we inform him personally before we enforce our warrant with the police.'

There was a small coffee shop opposite the justice ministry and we made our way there to wait for Alissa.

My nerves were getting the better of me and I couldn't bear just sitting around on my butt when I felt that something was wrong – to my mind, things just weren't adding up.

'I'm going to take a walk,' I said. 'I'm tired of doing nothing and can't just sit around any more.'

I walked back towards the ministry of justice, my camera bag over my shoulder. A side street with a boom control station led to the building. People passed through the boom and made their way down a flight of stairs to the main entrance to the building which Alissa had entered. Feeling uneasy about the young soldier's earlier remarks to Monique, I decided to hang around the entrance in anticipation of Alissa's return. If this was a trap of some sort she would most likely be escorted out of the building by police or soldiers. If this happened, I could simply turn around and go back to Phillip and Monique at the coffee shop.

I was cleared by the guards at the boom station and started pacing up and down the small stretch of road that ran behind the ministry of justice. I had opened the lid of my camera bag to take out my notebook when I heard someone yelling at me. I turned in his direction and saw two soldiers approaching, their rifles trained on me. They moved slowly, their knees bent as if they were expecting an aggressive reaction from me. Startled by this sudden turn of events, I raised my hands in the air and said, 'Hold on! What did I do?'

'Take your bag off your shoulder slowly,' the first soldier said. 'If you don't do as I say I will shoot.'

'No problem,' I said slowly lifting the sling off my shoulder and placing the bag on the ground. I had hardly done so when the two men lunged forward at me. I hit the ground chest first and they grabbed my hands and forced them behind my back. One soldier shoved his knee into my neck as if to prevent me from looking round.

'What did I do?' I gasped. They had knocked the wind out of me.

'What is in your bag?'

'Just a video camera.'

The soldier ripped the bag open and removed the camera, switching it on to see for himself whether I was telling the truth.

'What are you doing here?' he asked angrily.

'I am waiting for my friend who is inside the building,' I said. 'I didn't know that I was trespassing. You cleared me at the boom.' A wave of relief washed over me when I realised that the soldiers only suspected me of being a terrorist and that this was not part of the trap I had been imagining. Then again, being suspected of terrorism is not exactly a good thing either.

'Okay, you can get up and leave this place now,' the soldier said waiting for me to get up and move ahead of them towards the boom station.

I was happy to rejoin Phillip and Monique at the coffee shop with my aching neck.

'Where have you been?' Phillip asked, noticing that I was a bit shaken.

'Tasting soldiers' boots,' I answered, too embarrassed to go into details.

Just then Alissa crossed the road and came towards us.

'Good news,' she said. 'The paperwork is in place and we can go across the street to the police.'

Our mood was upbeat, to say the least. Finally, we thought, we were one step ahead of Hajjar.

We were well received at the police station and officers were quickly dispatched to make the arrests. A few sarcastic comments about our mission were made from time to time, but none that didn't bounce off our thick hides. The plan was to get the owners to the police station and threaten them with prison if they didn't disclose the whereabouts of the chimps. Trading in endangered species was illegal and the fact that they owned some had to be accounted for.

The captain in charge assured us that the Lebanese police were not to be messed with and that they had 'ways and means' of getting the information they wanted. After about three hours the first owner arrived. His name was Emile Hamieh and he was the bastard who kept the chimpanzee Ricardo in the small cage at his gas station. Next to arrive was Naifeh who was accompanied by several men all of whom resembled Salim in one way or another. Their arrival in a yellow Hummer H2 impressed bystanders but did nothing to move us as we stared at them from the steps of the police station, pleased at last that we seemed to be getting somewhere. Tony Chamoun, the owner of the zoo, was the last to arrive.

The 'interrogations' took several hours but eventually we were called into a room. The captain proceeded to give us disturbing news that would shatter our hopes of rescuing the chimpanzees. We were shown two photographs of two different chimps wrapped in garbage bags. Naifeh and Hamieh both claimed that their chimps were dead, one shot after trying to escape and the other dying from a mysterious illness. The fate of Ricardo seemed indisputable as his wounds, visible in the photos, were evidence of his violent death. Naifeh's chimp, however, looked as if it could have been drugged and then placed in a garbage bag.

I refused to accept that this could be called justice. Surely there must be some way the owners could be held accountable? Accountable, in the first instance, for being in possession of endangered species and in Hamieh's case for having admitted to killing his chimp. But killing primates, other than humans, didn't constitute murder in that or any other part of the world.

It all reeked of Hajjar's involvement, but there was no evidence to support this. It seemed that Hajjar was in the group that had arrived at the same time as Naifeh and it was he who was negotiating with the police on behalf of Naifeh and Hamieh. There was nothing that tied Hajjar to any of the owners but the fact that he had shown up at the police station suggested that he was assisting them. Did he have to solve their problems because he had sold the primates to them illegally? Tony Chamoun used his zoo permits to explain his ownership of the chimp, although technically he had still purchased the animal illegally. This permit system wasn't bulletproof – far from it. If the animal was born in Lebanon it would not require a CITES permit since it had not been imported from any of the countries that were CITES signatories. Only a Lebanese permit would be required but neither Naifeh nor Hamieh was in possession of one. This infringement only incurred a small fine. Naifeh and Hamieh could be charged with possession of an endangered species since neither had the required permit to keep them.

This was the beginning of the end of our mission to Lebanon and what followed happened so quickly that it made my head spin. The police captain, who had been summoned by the general prosecutor, returned and asked us to leave the building with him for an 'open air' discussion. Hajjar was standing outside. Oozing confidence, it was clear that he was going to try to intimidate us. I would finally look him in the eye; this man we had been pursuing for days was standing in front of us, but h.e was far from being in police handcuffs.

The captain gathered us together with Hajjar standing only feet away from us grinning infuriatingly as though he knew something we didn't.

'There are other ways to handle this,' he said, avoiding eye contact. 'Financially more interesting ways. He has offered us more than five thousand dollars. How much do you have?'

'Excuse me?' Monique and Alissa were dumbfounded.

So Hajjar had again managed to get a step ahead of us. How would we, as an NGO, fare in a bidding war with a notorious smuggler and drug dealer? No too good, was my guess.

'Maybe ten thousand,' said the captain. 'Maybe more.'

'We're done here,' I said. 'Let's go.'

'Suit yourself,' the captain said. 'Sorry I couldn't help.'

As I ushered the group through the palisades I gave Hajjar one last look of defiance. Making his intentions plain, he raised his thumb to his throat and slowly drew it across from side to side. Not only were two of the three chimps dead, but we might be next. We needed to get away quickly because not only had we lost the support of the police but we had also been threatened by a man who, I had no doubt whatsoever, was capable of murder.

'We don't have to worry about our personal safety,' said Monique when I voiced my concern. 'We have the protection of Salim and my father is also armed.'

'Great!' I burst out. 'On the run from a drug dealer and under the protection of a terrorist!'

Of course our safety was paramount, but part of me didn't want to accept that we had lost this fight, and were ultimately abandoning the chimps. We had come so far and to have to walk away lamely at the end didn't seem right. Good always triumphs over evil, they say, but only if good has more determination than evil has cunning.

I wasn't afraid of Hajjar. I just didn't have the means to take him on. It could be just a matter of time before Hajjar tried to carry out his threat and there was no point in endangering anyone. What I was uncomfortable with was that we'd be leaving Monique and Alissa behind when we returned to South Africa.

'I can't believe they just murdered two chimps,' Phillip said, shaking his head in disbelief.

'That's because they didn't,' I replied. 'The chimps are alive and I want to prove it. I've had enough of this bullshit cat-and-mouse game. So if the chimps are dead as far as the authorities are concerned …'

'… then if we find them we won't be in trouble for confiscating them because we have the valid CITES permits,' Phillip finished my sentence for me.

'You guys are crazy!' Alissa said, puzzled and angry at the same time. 'Did you miss the part where Hajjar threatened to kill you?'

'We need to do two things,' I said. 'First, we need to make sure that Hajjar doesn't carry out his threat when we are gone and, secondly, we need to get the chimps if they are still alive. Call Salim, please, Alissa. We can make one last attempt to save the chimps.' I pleaded with her, knowing full well the implications of the road I was about to choose.

Alissa thought about it for a few moments, looking at me in the rear-view mirror. 'Okay.'

It wasn't long before she had Salim on the phone and had what seemed to be a short and to the point conversation with him.

We met Salim a little after 5pm. He was driving a black 500E Mercedes Benz and was once again accompanied by the nondescript-looking man who had come to the zoo with him. They both looked as intimidating as before.

'You come alone,' Salim said to me.

I didn't answer. I simply unslung my camera bag from my shoulder and handed it to Phillip. 'I don't know who I can trust any more,' I told him. If you don't hear from me before midnight call my brother and get out of the country ASAP.'

I knew that between my brother and father all hell would break loose if they had to come to Lebanon to look for me.

'You sure about this?' Phillip asked. 'I have a bad feeling about it.'

'It's the only card left to play. You know I don't like losing a fight.'

I got into the back of the vehicle and we drove off rapidly.

'So, you decided to take me up on my offer?' Salim asked. 'What do you want to do?'

'There was one pet shop we visited yesterday where the owner said he would take us to see the chimps which were being kept only ten minutes away. I want the swine to take us there. The shop had an Arabic name which I don't know how to pronounce, but here's the address.' I ripped the page out of my notebook and gave it to Salim.

'This place is not nearby,' Salim said and gave his driver instructions. It took us about forty minutes to get to the shop. The driver parked some distance away, but not so far that we didn't have a clear view of it. The large roller doors were open and the owner was still tending to the animals in their cages.

'Now what?' I asked.

'Now we wait until he wants to close the doors.'

We sat there waiting, just staring at the shop.

'I checked you out, you know,' Salim said, breaking the silence.

'What do you mean?'

'I made sure yours was not a family of infidels.'

'Infidels?'

'Americans, or westerners. Your people are much the same as us.'

I was thinking, how on earth did I get myself into this shit? Here I was, sitting in a car having a theological discussion with two terrorists who wouldn't hesitate to dispose of me if I said or did anything out of line. I checked the position of the door handle in case I said the wrong thing and had to get out quick. Monique had told me that Salim was sincere, but he was none the less trained to be ruthless and unpredictable.

'Are you referring to Afrikaners?' I asked.

'Yes. You fought the British.'

'That was a long time ago.'

'That doesn't change anything,' he said.

Trying to change the topic as quickly as possible, I simply agreed. 'We kicked their asses in battle, if that counts for anything.'

'That's right,' Salim said. 'Did you know that I can never see my family again? There is only one way out of our organisation – to die a martyr. Or be sent to a special prison. You can never go back to your family.'

Salim was opening up to me. I wondered what the hell for.

'I have a wife and a child,' he continued. 'I can't see them again.'

I really didn't know what to say, so I did the next best thing. I shut up. I knew how bad the consequences could be if I stepped in my mouth.

At about 7pm the owner of the pet shop walked to the doors and started to roll them down.

'It's time to go!' They were out of the car in a flash.

I had no idea how this was going to turn out, but I wasn't intending to cut anyone's fingers off. I was hoping the owner would do one of two things: he would have enough respect for the two men, once they had explained who they were, to tell them where the chimps were, and that he'd later relay a message to Hajjar to tell him that BETA members were not involved.

Salim and his friend ducked in under the steel doors that were only half closed. I followed in time to hear the owner's protests. But there was no confrontation. Salim began to speak in a very calm, measured voice, more as though he was shopping for a puppy than looking to break bones. The conversation that followed lacked the aggression that I had been expecting. Then a surprising thing happened. Salim bowed at the owner and ushered me out of the shop.

'What's happening?' I asked when we were outside.

'We can't touch him,' Salim said. 'He is a Muslim elder and he is part of Hezbollah.'

'Fuck this!' I yelled in frustration. 'Give me a break!'

'Let it go, Eugene. You are not meant to leave with the chimps.'

Easier said than done. A few uncomfortable moments followed as I refused to accept that this was the end of the line. We had lost and the chimps were doomed.

As we drove back to the apartment a silence fell over us. Enough silence for me to be able to think. In a way I was angry that I had lost. In a way I was also ashamed for being willing to go as far as I had. Would I have stopped Salim from using anything other than verbal intimidation? Anger clouds judgement and I was full of anger. These were demons I'd have to face sometime.

Salim dropped me off in front of Monique's apartment and I made my way up in the elevator. They were all there, anxious to know what had happened.

'I am sorry,' I said. 'There was nothing I could do. We've lost.'

Everyone slumped despondently in their chairs, trying to deal with their disappointment.

Eventually, Phillip said, 'Well, we did what we could.'

'I can't believe I let them win,' I said, fighting back tears.

'I think you did enough.'

The next day we left Beirut. Despite our frustration, we had made new friends and a spirit of camaraderie had grown among us. Moreover, Monique and Alissa were convinced they had nothing to fear from Hajjar.

And so my first rescue mission had failed, but the experience taught me valuable lessons that would be put to use on many other, successful missions. We had not yet boarded our plane when Phillip received an unexpected phone call. As he hung up he smiled at me and said, 'Well, we might be going home without the chimps, but our work's not over. As soon as we get home we have to relocate three problem chimps from the Johannesburg Zoo.'

'Damn!' I replied. 'We travel halfway across the world trying to rescue chimps, only to find that there are some in our own backyard that need saving!'

We might have left Lebanon with heavy hearts, but we knew that other chimps would need us in the future and we would be there.

SIX

THE FIRST ARRIVALS

In truth, it was the legal system of Lebanon that led to our failure. Mark had encountered a corrupt bureaucracy and it wasn't surprising that the mission was doomed. We would never have been able to come up with a strategy that would have yielded a different result. Lebanon had a long way to go before it would be able to stamp out trafficking in endangered animals.

Although the experience created a bond among those of us who had lived through it together, it was difficult to explain to the people back home just exactly what went wrong in Lebanon. The expenses incurred on the mission were enormous as we had flown three adult size cages to Lebanon only to have to abandon them there as the cost of bringing them home again – empty – was too high. I took responsibility for the failed mission but needless to say JGI South Africa wasn't too pleased about the outcome. Our rescue work had only just begun and I knew I wouldn't get away with another such failure. From that point on we would insist on controlling all aspects of a mission ourselves.

We were encouraged to continue with our efforts in Angola; Sally and a number of other chimps were still waiting for the Angolan government to decide their fate. It seemed that humans were always to be the chimpanzee's worst enemy. Since our departure for Lebanon another group had taken it upon themselves to intervene in our Angolan rescue attempts, saying that our contribution had not been good enough and that they would do better. This group was the international organisation called the Great Ape Project (GAP).

As I reacquainted myself with the accumulated papers on my desk, I came across a fax that was highly significant. It conveyed a message from the department of forestry in Angola in which we were informed that they had postponed any relocation of chimpanzees to South Africa, preferring to investigate a possible relationship with GAP Brazil. I felt as though I had been punched in the guts when I realised that GAP Brazil had inadvertently halted all the progress we had made in negotiations with Angola. The fax stated further that GAP Brazil had taken chimps from Angola on previous occasions and that they were willing to raise the amount of money required by the department of forestry. What GAP Brazil had not realised was that their intervention had lifted the pressure on the Angolan authorities. This could translate to further delays in relocating the chimpanzees while the Angolans considered whether they could negotiate better terms with GAP Brazil. Further delays could only be detrimental to the chimpanzees.

Everyone involved, including PASA, had up to this point firmly believed that the welfare and relocation of chimpanzees from Angola should not be tied to any fee demanded by the government. Now the arrival of GAP Brazil at the negotiation table had changed the situation and they were effectively blocking us from moving forward to rescue Sally and the other Luanda chimps.

All I could do was voice our disapproval to GAP and Dr Almeida but it seemed that common interests between the two of them were strong enough to bring the negotiations with Chimp Eden to a halt. The relocation of all the Angolan chimpanzee orphans was extremely urgent as some of them were facing certain death if action was not taken soon; furthermore, Brazil as their destination would send the wrong signal to the international conservation community who were looking closely at the conservation ethics of the post-war Angolan government.

Meanwhile, we had an urgent matter to deal with. You will recall that just before we left Lebanon Phillip had received a phone call asking him to relocate three chimpanzees from the Johannesburg Zoo. Three adult males – Amadeus, Abu and Nikki – had been involved in a serious altercation with other more dominant individuals in their group. They had now become a liability for the zoo which was anxious to avoid a similar incident that might possibly have more dire consequences. The plan was simple: we would take our remaining wooden crates up to the zoo, load the chimps with the help of zoo staff and relocate them in the first garden enclosure and sleeping quarters that had been completed at Chimp Eden. This sounded like a walk in the park compared with what we had gone through in Lebanon, but once again I was wrong.

The Johannesburg Zoo staff took charge of loading the chimpanzees, but we found that there were only two crates in the back of the truck. The reason, we were told, was that Amadeus had sustained some injuries that would take a week or more to heal, and only then would he be ready for transport. Neither Phillip nor I considered the implications of moving the chimps at two different times, as in itself it didn't seem a significant issue.

I was extremely excited. The fact that this landmark zoo needed the help of a small sanctuary that was just starting out was a moment of pride for me. As anticipated, we returned to the sanctuary without a hitch and proceeded to offload the first crate. Its occupant was glued to the vent in the crate, staring out at the crowd of staff and family who had come to share the great moment.

Eventually the crates were placed against a hatch that opened into the garden enclosure. It was a memorable moment as each chimp got the opportunity to leave the confines of their crates and explore their new sleeping quarters. They must have realised that this was a new beginning for both of them. Looking a bit shell shocked, they inspected the interior of the sleeping quarters, jumping up against the window bars, calling out loudly and excitedly, and then listening to hear if there would be a response from other chimpanzees. Excitement was not the only emotion they showed; they were both insecure and from time to time this was revealed in their facial expressions, gritting their teeth and reaching out to each other with open hands. If only we could have explained what was awaiting them!

The next two weeks were spent developing a routine for both the chimps and for us. For the chimps it was going out into the enclosure in the morning, learning when it was feeding time, and returning to the sleeping quarters at night. The garden enclosure was smaller than the one they had been used to at the Johannesburg Zoo at around 1 200 square feet, but the amount of attention they received more than compensated for the temporary lack of space. Abu was the brute of the two, constantly rocking his head from side to side as if suffering from some neurological disorder and then usually following this up with an aggressive display, rocking on all fours with his hair erect.

During this time I myself felt as though I was suffering from some disorder and its main symptom was paranoia. I worried all the time about the possibility of the chimps escaping, and Abu's violent displays didn't exactly put my fears to rest. Phillip, on the other hand, knew the chimps intimately having raised them at the zoo from the time they arrived there twelve years earlier.

The two males shared similar histories: both were orphaned by the bush meat trade and both were rescued by the same man, Professor Peter Grey, as part of a JGI South Africa rescue. This, however, was where the similarities ended. Nikki was a clever, cunning and calculating chimpanzee who spent a lot of time thinking of ways to instigate trouble. Raised to be part of a human household, Nikki was taught to eat with a knife and fork, to sleep in a bed and to wear human clothes until such time as the owner could no longer cope with Nikki's longing to become the true primate he was. He was also a lot smaller than Abu which put him at a considerable disadvantage during a fight. It's possible that all these factors played a part in his learning to use brain rather than brawn to solve problems. In contrast, Abu was physically big and had a face that would scare most small children. He used his size to intimidate Nikki and always got what he wanted.

The two of them settled into a routine and I spent most of my time with Phillip, learning how a sanctuary should be run. Phillip had had considerable experience working with primates and other species at the zoo, but in some ways this was also a new experience for him. It was the first time he had had a sanctuary to manage with large, vegetation-covered enclosures ready to put at the disposal of uncontrollable intelligent primates. However, he showed not an ounce of fear, never hesitating to demonstrate his dominance to the two chimps, even though they could be enormously intimidating at times. I learned that 'never back down' and 'never show fear' were two key principles in gaining their respect. Sometimes, standing up close to the bars when Abu decided to display, I would instinctively jump back to protect myself, but Phillip stood firm every time.

About two weeks after Abu and Nikki arrived it was time to relocate Amadeus. Described as a big chimp with a small heart by Phillip, I hoped he would bring some balance to the rather unstable party of two. Moving Amadeus proceeded pretty much as the relocation of the first two had – the zoo staff were efficient and we were on our way in no time at all.

Since this was now a practised routine, I had come up with the idea that when we arrived at Chimp Eden we should introduce Amadeus and his companions to the media and so I had organised news cameras to join us in hailing the opening of South Africa's first chimpanzee sanctuary. It didn't occur to me that things might not work out as planned, nor did I acknowledge the fact that if anything *should* go wrong it would be broadcast nationwide on South Africa's main news channel at the time. I was confident that the staff was well trained and totally familiar with the procedures we had devised to deal with an emergency, which I quite frankly did not expect to happen.

Soon after we arrived the crate containing Amadeus was moved up against the outdoor hatch of the sleeping quarters and I gave the news cameras and photographers a broad smile as I lifted up the door and reunited Amadeus with his friends. There was instant recognition among the three of them: Amadeus submitted to Abu and Nikki gave the newcomer a bear hug. The cameras rolled through the Plexiglass windows and from the expressions on the faces of those witnessing the spectacle of primate friendship, we were all sharing a heart-warming moment. But this was the point where the fairytale ended and the nightmare began. Not seeing a problem with putting on an extra special show, we decided to go one step further and open the hatch so that all three chimps could emerge from their sleeping quarters into the open enclosure.

Eugene with Sally (on his back) and Joao. During the early days in the 'Infant Camp' Eugene spent time on an almost daily basis helping the chimps to develop trust between each other (Natasha Cussons)

Eugene trying to calm Lika before darting her on
the night of her rescue in Luanda (Lucinda Piets)

Lika immobilised in her crate before leaving for the airport (Lucinda Piets)

Cozy in his cage in the trailer in Ancona. His skin is pale because he has not seen sunlight for three years (Eugene Cussons)

Cozy inspecting the quarantine quarters at Chimp Eden (Phillip Cronje)

Cozy, Sally and Zeena with Eugene during introductions in quarantine (Eugene Cussons)

Eugene and Marco in the Sudan. Eugene found it helped to gain respect from the dominant chimp by climbing with him (Friosphere Productions)

Eugene meeting Azzi and Dinka for the first
time in their makeshift quarters at Sue Knight's
halfway house (Triosphere Productions)

Nikki peeling the bark off a jacaranda tree during the first week after his introduction into the 'big' enclosure (Francois Theron)

Amadeus enjoying some fruit (Francois Theron)

Cozy, Keeper Jonathan and Sally at feeding time. Jonathan was one of the first keepers to start work at Chimp Eden and he has built a trusting relationship with Cozy, Sally and Zeena (Eugene Cussons)

The news crew asked for some background commentary and I was happy to oblige, positioning myself at the opposite end of the garden enclosure. Then, as we all watched, the sleeping quarters hatch was opened and the three chimps leapt out into the open. Abu immediately started his usual aggressive display, ripping up tufts of grass and throwing handfuls at us. Amadeus was not pleased with Abu's behaviour and dashed towards a part of the fence that separated the garden court from their future enclosure. The new enclosure, already completed, was not to be unveiled for another two weeks so the power to the electric fences had not been switched on. I saw Amadeus gazing up and down one of the fence poles and with a shock I realised that the outcome was inevitable. Time seemed to slow down, or perhaps my mind just did not want to accept what my eyes were relaying to it. Amadeus grabbed the fence pole and moved up it in a single swift movement. The news cameras panned over to the events that were now unfolding, getting a profile of my face in with the image of Amadeus leaping up the pole in the background.

'Oh shit!' came the words from my unguarded mouth. There may be many other words in the English language to describe a moment of panic like this, but I doubt if any of them would have been more apt or to the point. The only problem was that this was all caught on camera.

Amadeus was now sitting on the wall overlooking his home-to-be. He appeared to be quite calm, but it only took one glance from him to produce instant hysteria among the assembled media and cameras. I instinctively jumped on to the wall to gain a better vantage point and shouted loudly to get everyone's attention.

'No need to panic! Just follow me!'

But few of them hung around to hear my reassuring message; they were already running down the road towards their cars. The few who had listened lined up behind me and I led them towards the day visit centre, which was the emergency protocol laid down for guests in the event of possible danger to them. With me were a few guides who helped to usher everyone to the restaurant, a 'lockdown' area which was in the building furthest away from the 'escaped' Amadeus.

But Amadeus wasn't really interested in scaring people and soon climbed down into the enclosure that was rightfully his. Phillip reacted quickly and went immediately to the enclosure gate in order to reach Amadeus. Once the guests were all secured inside the restaurant I rushed back the top enclosure as fast as possible. My fears, although warranted, proved unfounded. Panting heavily from exertion, I was witness to a truly special moment. Walking slowly along the boundary of the enclosure came Amadeus. He was clutching a handful of African daisies, pausing every so often to sniff at the flowers. He made his way to a guava tree, which happened to be in season, and plucked a few pieces of fruit from it. Then he happily lay down on his back – it was as though the flowers and fruit were things he had been longing for all his life. I was strangely moved. Phillip and my brother John had entered the enclosure and were now close to Amadeus. I was quite surprised that John had followed Phillip but he probably felt compelled to do so as back-up, bearing in mind that there were still quite a few media guests on the property.

With the situation more or less under control, I continued with the next part of the protocol which was to inform our standby veterinarian to dispatch a vet crew to Chimp Eden without delay. We needed them to immobilise Amadeus so that he could be moved back to his sleeping quarters. The veterinarians, who were located in the nearby town of Nelspruit, had considerable wildlife experience, but they had never had to immobilise a chimp before and we all ran the risk of being attacked by Amadeus if he objected to the procedure.

The crew arrived fifteen minutes later and while Amadeus had his feet up, enjoying all that nature had to offer, the vets prepared two immobilising darts. The Dan-Inject rifle they used was state of the art. It used carbon dioxide gas under pressure to launch a feathered dart accurately at distances of up to 50 feet. We now had to come up with a strategy that would enable us to get close to Amadeus without raising his suspicions that something was about to happen. Chimpanzees have a sixth sense when it comes to veterinarians, and Phillip had warned us that chimps were no fools and were quickly alerted to anything they perceived to be out of the ordinary.

The veterinarian who would be doing the darting was Dr Ferreira du Plessis and even though he'd had tons of experience darting rhinos, this would be a first for him. It was not simply a matter of strolling up to a chimpanzee weighing 140 pounds and producing the rifle with ample time to take aim and shoot. We had to make a plan to conceal the rifle, only exposing it at the last moment when Amadeus was suitably distracted.

'Hide the gun in your jacket and walk behind me,' I said to Ferreira. 'Amadeus knows me and won't be alarmed. If you walk up to him with the rifle in plain sight you're going to be in trouble – not to mention Phillip and John who are standing alongside him.'

'Okay,' Ferreira replied. 'At what distance will we be shooting?'

'I can get you right up to the fence, which should make it a 20-foot shot.'

'Right, we're set,' said Ferreira, wiping a fresh bead of sweat from his face.

With the Dan-Inject rifle charged for short range, the vet and his assistant Albertus followed me, the gun and its 18-inch barrel concealed in the sleeve of a green jacket. We walked slowly, Ferreira with one hand on my shoulder and the jacket pointing to the ground. We were within nine feet of the fence when the shot went off. I felt the burst of carbon dioxide brushing against my trousers, but I kept my eyes firmly fixed on Amadeus, waiting for his reaction. The chimp, startled by the shot, looked up at the three of us. We remained absolutely still and, not finding anything suspicious about us, Amadeus settled down again on his patch of lush grass. Only then did the three of us look down at the dart lying right next to my left foot.

I looked at Ferreira in disbelief.

'Shit,' he said, wiping his brow again. 'I'm sorry.'

'I hope you can load again without raising Amadeus's suspicions,' I said as I watched the chimp settle back happily, eating his guavas and sniffing his bunch of flowers.

I looked at Phillip who was staring at me, a puzzled look on his face. I nodded at him and waited for Ferreira to tell me he was ready. Finally, he tapped me on the shoulder to indicate that he was ready for round two and we once more began to move closer to the fence.

As we reached the fence, I whispered: 'I'm going to signal to Phillip and John that we are ready for the shot.'

'Okay.' He slowly removed the rifle from the sleeve of the jacket.

Acknowledging my nod, Phillip called out to Amadeus, trying to draw his attention away from us. He then started walking quickly in the opposite direction. John followed in the same direction where there was an escape route through the enclosure gate in case things went wrong. Amadeus was so relaxed in his surroundings that he barely lifted his head. This was Ferreira's chance and he slowly lifted the rifle and rested it on my shoulder. After what seemed to be only a second's delay, the burst of carbon dioxide left the muzzle and the dart raced between the wires of the fence and struck Amadeus in the leg.

Amadeus sat up instantly and plucked at the dart which was firmly lodged in his upper right leg. The dart was designed with a barb that would lodge beneath the skin, ensuring that its contents were injected under pressure into the muscle before the animal had the chance to pull it out. The negative side of this was that the barb was so effective that it mostly needed a small incision to remove it. Although calm, Amadeus was plucking furiously at the dart as Phillip and John made their way out of the enclosure.

Amadeus managed to remove the dart and stared at it in disgust, sniffing curiously at the point of the needle that had painfully pierced his leg. Then he put the dart down, picked up his flowers and continued to walk down the line of the fence. We were still standing on the opposite side of the fence and instinctively moved with Amadeus as he began his walk. Fortunately, he hadn't noticed where the dart had come from as Ferreira had been quick to hide the gun behind me.

'Leave the gun on the ground,' I said. 'I'm guessing that he'll be unhappy with you if he notices that you were the one who shot him.'

'I think I'd rather go back to the car and prepare another dart, just in case.' He turned away, hiding the rifle in the jacket.

Albertus, the second veterinarian, and I continued to trail Amadeus who now looked as though he was starting to get drowsy. Eventually he could go no further and he sat down under a big acacia. Phillip and John had already organised the next step, which was to get a vehicle inside the enclosure so that Amadeus could be loaded for a speedy transit to the quarantine building, the only facility where we could take him to ensure that there wasn't another attempt to 'escape'. Phillip was ready to drive into the enclosure in his Land Rover pickup truck and we dashed back to him. Time was of the essence as there was no telling how long Amadeus would remain unconscious.

Amadeus, sound asleep, was loaded on to the pickup and we drove quickly to the quarantine building where he was transferred into a secure cage. I breathed a sigh of relief. Proper training and good teamwork had ensured that a possible disaster had been averted. Things might have had a different outcome if a more aggressive chimp had been involved.

The 'escape' was the top story on television news in South Africa. Amadeus had achieved his fifteen seconds of fame, while my hopes of looking professional had been totally dashed. But although I might have embarrassed myself, the staff and our veterinarians had done Chimp Eden proud by acting quickly and according to protocol.

We would move Amadeus back to the chimps' sleeping quarters the next day to be reunited with Abu and Nikki. We made minor changes to the fence of the garden enclosure so that we wouldn't have a repeat performance and the next day the vets returned to help Phillip and me move Amadeus back to his two companions. That also turned into a day to remember.

The events of that day will be for ever burned into my memory as one of the closest shaves I have had with death. That's quite a statement from someone who does accelerated free fall skydiving for fun! Under the illusion that Amadeus was a mild-tempered chimp, we devised a simple strategy to lure him into a wooden transport crate that we would position against the door of the quarantine cage into which the sleeping Amadeus had been unloaded the day before. But there was a serious weakness in the design of the quarantine cages, one that could have cost my life or the life of any of my team members.

The transport crate was only about four feet high, which was about three feet shorter than the door of the quarantine cage. This meant, of course, that there was an exposed area of about three feet above the top of the crate. The crate was designed so that its wooden door was lifted upwards, which would effectively close off the exposed area. The weakness? One had to sit on top of the wooden crate to lift the door from its sliding mountings and then hold the door in place against the quarantine cage.

Quite a test of one's bravery! They say that there is a fine line between bravery and stupidity but what they don't tell you is that the line is often blurred. The vets had to be in a position where they could immobilise Amadeus if he refused to enter the crate voluntarily. The plan was simple: open the hatch door between two adjacent quarantine cages, lure Amadeus through the hatch by offering him food, close the hatch behind him, and then lure him into the crate which will already be in position against the door of the second quarantine cage and will contain an abundance of enticing food. Simple.

Sitting on top of the crate and holding the crate door up, my face was literally an inch from the flexible mesh and bars set into the door. If the chimp became agitated and attempted to hit the mesh the crate door would strike me full in the face. My heart was pounding as I signalled to Phillip to open the hatch door between the cages. I imagined cage diving with great white sharks would feel something like this, except I had to hold one side of the cage in position. Phillip paused for a moment as though reassessing the plan and then he opened the hatch door.

Not hesitating for a moment, Amadeus eagerly charged through the hatch and settled down at the small pile of fruit in the centre of the cage. The hatch was closed behind him. Phillip and I both encouraged him in a calm, friendly tone and, indeed, he seemed quite relaxed. Then he noticed the additional pile of fruit stacked inside the crate and was about to investigate when he suddenly became suspicious and backed away. I was sitting only inches away from the crate door when he looked up at me and the flimsy door in the same way he had sized up the fence pole just before his escape the day before. A cold sweat broke out on my face as I realised that this chimp did not want to be manipulated and unfortunately for me I was standing between him and another walk in the great outdoors.

Amadeus started pacing up and down the cage, his raised hair indicating aggressive intent. He bobbed his head up and down as he became increasingly frustrated, and then he snapped and began running and jumping up against each wall of the cage and, inevitably, the door of the crate. He released a powerful punch and the cage door slammed into my face. My heart was pounding out of control but there was no escape for me. If I backed away he would jump out right on to my lap and possibly unleash his frustration on me. Fortunately the crate, which weighed around 265 pounds, was heavy enough to withstand the pounding that Amadeus was giving it. Realising that the situation was fast becoming one of potential disaster, Phillip reopened the hatch door hoping that Amadeus would move back, giving us time to come up with a different plan. But Amadeus was having none of it and continued with his furious display, pounding the walls so hard that I could feel every blow resonating through the crate door.

Phillip then put Plan B into action and opened up the water hose. He directed the massive blast of water at the ceiling creating an uncomfortable downpour over the cage and all of us. Water is sometimes used as a control measure when working with chimpanzees as they are not at all fond of it. But it didn't persuade Amadeus to move, only sufficing to make him even angrier. Eventually he settled down in the middle of the cage, panting with exertion. When I saw the expression on his face I reckoned that this was it: he was going to find a way to escape and he was going to kill me for frustrating him. I looked up at my hands, now shaking with adrenalin and exhaustion and thought that if only I'd had some heavy string or rope I could have tied the crate to the door frame of the quarantine cage, which would at least have given me a few moments to escape. No such luck.

Then, in a clearly calculated move, Amadeus pushed himself up against the far wall of the cage and launched himself forward, kicking the crate door with all his force. Time seemed to slow down as the crate was violently flung backwards and slammed against the opposite wall of the corridor. In a single movement, Amadeus punched and dislodged the crate door from its mountings and both he and the door came crashing down on me. In what can only have been a reflex action, I shoved the crate door, with Amadeus on top of it, to my left, my burst of energy no doubt the result of huge doses of adrenalin surging through me.

The instinct for survival took over as I rolled to the right, falling on the soaking floor and struggling to get to my feet. Phillip had dropped the hose. Fortunately, he was also standing to the right of the cage. The two of us rushed through the exit door hoping that Amadeus wouldn't compose himself quickly enough to pursue us. Only then did I become aware that something was missing: the two veterinarians! Phillip came to this realisation at the same moment as I did and we yelled to them simultaneously. They answered from a cage on the opposite side of the corridor. When things started getting out of control they had both leapt into a vacant cage and secured the lock … which could easily be opened from the outside. It would have been no problem for Amadeus to have opened the lock …

Fortunately, Amadeus decided to go in the opposite direction. The Plexiglass at the end of the corridor provided a great outside view and he seemed to have been attracted to this as a possible escape route. Escape, not murder, seemed to be his priority.

'Get out!' Phillip yelled at the vets.

Ferreira and Albertus hesitated as though there was some sort of security behind the bars of the cage.

'Get out now before he comes this way!' I shouted.

This time they mustered up the guts to leave the cage. Slipping and sliding like two drunks across the wet floor they managed to stumble through the door to safety.

Once we were safely out of harm's way I slid to the floor, my back against the wall, weak with relief. In the moment that Amadeus had slammed into the crate door I had accepted my fate. I would never see Natasha again, never see the sanctuary come into its own. Happily, fate had different plans for me and I was shaken but unscathed. Drained and panting, the four of us looked at one another and someone started to chuckle. As for me, I promised myself that I would never again be caught without a piece of string ... And since that day I have always looped a piece of string around my left leg before leaving home. It has saved my life on more than one occasion.

An hour later we returned with enough drugs to tranquillise a rhino and we successfully immobilised Amadeus and then reunited him with Abu and Nikki. He never tried to escape again.

SEVEN

THE ITALIAN STALLION

After the chaos of Amadeus's escape, life at the sanctuary began to settle into a comfortable routine. Each day the four keepers, Phillip and I would busy ourselves with cleaning, sourcing chimp food, construction and general caretaking tasks. After two weeks of continuous construction and testing we finally opened the first large outdoor enclosure and sleeping quarters.

It was another occasion I shall never forget. The Three Stooges, as I had started calling them, were beside themselves with excitement when the gate between the garden enclosure and their new home was opened. Each reacted differently to the event. Abu ran around the boundary fence until he had exhausted himself; Nikki busied himself exploring the treetops, eventually getting himself entangled in a thorn tree, much to his annoyance; and Amadeus finally had access to what he wanted so badly – flowers, fruit and open space – but, strangely, he just climbed the nearest tree and stayed there for most of the day.

The need for rescue missions also became more pressing with several potential rescue cases arising at this time. There was Joao, a fifty-five-year-old chimpanzee from Mozambique, as well as Zeena, an infant chimpanzee in the United Arab Emirates. Joao was a particularly sad case. Having been left at the Maputo Zoo more than fifty years ago, he had seen the Mozambique conflict come and go, as well as other animals that didn't survive the difficult conditions during the war. Several relocation attempts had failed over the years. Zeena, on the other hand, had only recently been confiscated in Dubai. Fortunately for her, a British veterinarian living and working in the UAE was taking care of her and handling all the logistical stumbling blocks to get her relocated.

Another case that was becoming urgent was that of a chimpanzee that I would later nickname the 'Italian Stallion'. Jane Goodall had always been an ardent supporter of the sanctuary and the role it was to play in the cause of international conservation. It was at her request that I investigated this case which would fundamentally affect my views on the relationship between animals and human beings. Jane Goodall's assistant Mary Lewis forwarded me an urgent email from Jane detailing the assistance needed by JGI Italy. The email explained that JGI Italy had sent the same request to several other orphanages but none of them were capable of rescuing the chimpanzee in the immediate future. The chimpanzee's physical condition was the reason why he needed to be rescued quickly. According to the veterinarian who had examined Cozy, as the chimp was named, he had lost a considerable amount of muscle mass, was extremely emaciated and wouldn't survive another six months in his present circumstances. His mental condition was described as unstable and it was virtually impossible for anyone other than his owner to enter the trailer where he was kept.

I was keen to investigate the request from Jane. However, Chimp Eden was originally intended to rescue chimpanzees from war-torn countries in Africa and if we were to become part of a larger conservation initiative alongside other organisations then rescuing a chimpanzee out of Italy could compromise the ethics of the sanctuary. Then again, the core reason for the existence of the sanctuary was to rescue chimps and offer them quality of life, and bureaucracy should not be allowed to stand in the way of this. At least, that was how I saw it.

I phoned the head of JGI Italy, Mrs Daniela De Donno, and she reiterated the urgency of the case. Cozy's Israeli owner had lived in Ancona and had died a few years ago. Since then Cozy had been taken care of by the owner's partner, a Ms Svetlana. She had no experience in caring for chimpanzees and Cozy's condition had become so bad that she had turned to JGI Italy for help. The physical logistics and permit applications should be simple in comparison with other places from which we were trying to rescue chimps. The JGI South Africa team agreed that if we could do something then we should. With Angola in stalemate, there was nothing to stop me from helping Cozy, and so started the mission that would see me rescue our first chimpanzee. Phillip had established a very good connection for transit logistics, a company called GK Airfreight Service which was based in Frankfurt and specialised in animal transfers, handling the moving of anything from a cat to a race horse. They would provide the logistical cornerstone of the mission.

The joint effort between JGI Italy and JGI South Africa would have a simple plan. Cozy's blood samples would be taken by the veterinarian who had done his previous assessment. Overseen by JGI Italy, the samples would be sent from Rome to Amsterdam in The Netherlands. GK would build a crate according to the specifications of the Air

Transit Association and send it to Rome on Friday, 7 July 2006, transporting it via a trucking company from the airport to Ancona on 8 July. I would use the same veterinarian who had seen to the blood samples to immobilise Cozy for the truck trip back to Rome and the flight to South Africa on 9 July. Piece of cake.

If only everything in life worked according to plan …

The first problem to arise was the blood sampling. The veterinarian was only able to send the samples to Amsterdam seven days after they'd been taken. The late arrival of the blood was further hampered by the slow processing of the samples at the Biomedical Primate Research Centre which had promised to have the results with the South African state veterinarian on the day I arrived in Italy. Still, if the results were available by 4 July we would have enough time to get Cozy out on 9 July.

The samples dealt with, I asked Daniela to give me her reassurance that the export permits would be ready on my arrival and accordingly arranged for the CITES import permits, and I also made the necessary arrangements with the South African Veterinary Service to issue their import permits as soon as the blood results were available. With Phillip keeping an eye on the Three Stooges, I set off for Italy on my first solo mission. I had never been to Italy before and had no idea what to expect, and the prospect of having to deal with a chimpanzee that was apparently very aggressive didn't help to ease my nerves.

Mrs Monica Pace was the person who met me at Leonardo da Vinci Airport on behalf of JGI Italy on 3 July. Not quite five feet tall, my first impression of Monica was that she radiated cheerfulness and had a smile that could light up a room. It was summer in Europe and I relished the hot weather. Monica had located a hotel near the Colosseum for me and it didn't fail to make an impression. It wasn't just the charming little Hotel Nerva as much as the fact that it was located close to a historical marvel. I had to pinch myself to make sure I wasn't dreaming. I had come to Italy on a chimp rescue mission and, while the details of that were constantly on my mind, the surroundings couldn't have been more distracting. I would have loved to visit all the tourist attractions but my job wasn't about enjoying a foreign destination, it was about places and things you don't see on postcards. We had to get to work at once. Monica gave me time to check in to the hotel and then we made our way to the department of forestry to meet the CITES representative in Italy.

A friendly female official received us very courteously at the forestry offices and she reiterated their willingness to issue the permits and even their gratitude to Chimp Eden for rescuing Cozy. The permits were not ready yet but the official assured us that the paperwork wouldn't take more than a day to complete. I was urged to enjoy the sights of Rome while the documentation was being drawn up.

Things seemed to be going smoothly, too smoothly. However, this was Italy and if their officials were half as efficient as their sports cars then, in theory, everything should be a lot easier than it was in Africa. Was I going to get a break on this mission?

For the moment, I had nothing to do but wait. Seeing Cozy would also have to wait as Ancona, the town nearest to where he was being kept, was a few hours' drive from Rome. The blood results were expected to arrive from the Biomedical Primate Research Centre the next day, 4 July, and there would be ample time for me to remind the South African state veterinarian to approve, issue and forward me the veterinary import permit on the same day. The plan was still to leave with Cozy on a flight from Rome to Johannesburg on 9 July.

With such good fortune, I might even be able to enjoy myself in Rome on the Thursday and Friday before leaving for Ancona on the Saturday. It's rather mysterious how life never gives you a bone when you really deserve it. On the last few missions I had been dogged by misfortune; now, in Rome, would be the ideal moment for some good karma to come my way. I phoned Natasha that evening and told her that things couldn't be going better, but left out the part about my hotel room overlooking the wonders of ancient Rome. I always felt guilty about leaving her at home, yet I could never consider taking her on missions that might prove dangerous. But this seemed such an easy mission and the surroundings were wonderful.

Later, I made my way to the hotel dining room for dinner. The dining room and adjacent bar area were full of people staring excitedly at a television screen cheering what seemed to be a soccer game. I helped myself to a small table and a few minutes later a waiter appeared with a menu.

'What's all the excitement about?' I asked the waiter, gesturing towards the cheering crowd. 'A special game?'

'Yes, Italy is playing Germany. If we win, we go through to the Cup Final.'

'That's great … the Cup Final?' I asked thinking that it was just another European league match.

The young man hesitated, looking at me closely to determine whether or not I was pulling his leg. 'The … Soccer World Cup.'

'Oh yes, of course.' I faked as best I could. 'I did not know that the semi-final was tonight.'

'Yes, yes. We must win and play France in the final!'

I am not a soccer fan. The fact that my mission coincided with the Soccer World Cup had completely escaped me. Being in a part of the world that was fanatical about soccer, I could imagine that airports would be swamped with travelling fans. Fortunately, I wouldn't be travelling through Germany, the host country. Or so I thought.

That night I slept like a baby. This mission was nothing like the Lebanon trip when I hardly seemed to sleep at all. Wednesday morning arrived and since Italy was in the same time zone as South Africa I made a call to the South African state veterinarian's office to make sure they were on track with the issuing and forwarding of permits. They assured me that indeed they were and, with nothing to worry about, I decided to take a stroll through the streets of Rome. Without a guide and no real clue about where to go I just followed the flow of tourists. The Roman architecture was astounding and I was just starting to relax and enjoy myself when fate decided otherwise.

As I was admiring an ancient passageway lined on either side with gigantic pillars I got a call from a distressed Monica. Anticipating that she had something important to tell me, I found somewhere relatively quiet to take the call.

'Eugene, we have a problem,' she said.

'Okay, what's wrong?' I tried to remain calm, tried not to expect the worst.

'Where are you now? I will come and pick you up.'

'I'll meet you in front of the hotel,' I said. 'I'm just down the road.' I started off immediately in the direction of the hotel.

Endless possibilities for disaster and failure were running through my mind. The problem must be a significant one if Monica wanted to discuss it in person. I cursed under my breath as I made my way up the cobbled street. Was I jinxed? First Angola, and then Lebanon, and now ...?

Monica's dark blue Renault was waiting outside the hotel entrance. I knocked on the passenger window and then got into the car.

'What's the bad news?'

'Not so bad, but also not so good,' she said in her Italian-accented English. 'It seems that there are some processes that the forestry people have not completed but they are working on finishing the documentation.'

'So what is the bad news?'

'They don't know how long it will take.'

'Not even a guesstimate? Will it be done before the flight?'

'They can't tell me. I'm sorry, I don't know what to say because we were assured everything would be fine.'

'It's not your fault. I think the only thing we can do is apply a lot of pressure so that they realise the urgency of meeting the date of the flight.'

'Yes,' she answered. 'This I will do.'

'There is something you should know,' I said. 'The blood samples are valid for only twenty-one days and we are now on day seventeen. If the delay in issuing the permits takes too long the plan will fall through because we'll have to start the whole blood sampling process all over again.'

Monica immediately realised that postponement was not an option. 'I will phone them and tell them about this problem,' she said, picking up her mobile phone and dialling. After a short conversation she hung up and said: 'They are saying that we will just have to wait. There is nothing they can do.'

Once again, bureaucratic red tape had become the most difficult part of a mission. If only a mission could be as simple as feeding and taking care of the animal in transit! If we didn't have the permits by Friday morning, it was unlikely we'd catch our flight on the Sunday. The blood samples would no longer be valid and the mission would fail. A feeling of helplessness crept over me as I realised there wasn't much I could do about it. In Lebanon it had not been the officials but the animal owners who had foiled our rescue efforts; now it was the other way around.

Monica and I arranged to get together the next day to make another phone call to the ministry. The weekend was fast approaching. But we had no joy. The documentation was still not ready and we were advised to plan for an alternative date to relocate the chimpanzee. I was shattered. We had already spent more than $15 000 of donated money on this rescue attempt and once again it looked as though I'd be going home empty-handed. If I didn't return home with Cozy it would be the end of my short career as head of JGI South Africa's rescue team.

There wasn't much we could do except try to come up with ways of executing a follow-up mission. I knew that the likelihood of this happening was remote, but we decided to discuss this over lunch.

'You're right,' I said to Monica when she suggested we find a restaurant. 'I could do with a glass of red wine and a pizza.'

Monica arranged for her husband to pick us up at the hotel and we set off to a charming little restaurant near the Spanish Steps. The three of us enjoyed our lunch while trying to explore realistic options to overcome the problems that had so unexpectedly arisen. It was simply too costly to start from scratch. After lunch, Monica suggested we take a break from our problems and we walked to the Trevi Fountain which was crowded with tourists taking photographs and tossing coins into the water.

'What's that all about?' I asked pointing to a tourist who had just flipped a coin into the fountain.

'People believe that if you toss a coin into the water you will have good luck,' Monica answered with a cynical smile. 'Try it – we need all the help we can find!'

'I don't mind if I do,' I said. 'Although with my sort of luck the coin will clog the filter and ruin the fountain.'

I am not a superstitious person, yet I none the less found myself making a wish as I tossed a coin into the fountain. 'May we get Cozy safely back to Africa,' I said out loud, feeling a bit ridiculous. As we were leaving I picked up a leaflet lying on the ground and read that the actual belief was that if you tossed a coin into the fountain you would someday return to Rome. Nice thought – perhaps I would return with Cozy, and leave immediately for Africa.

As we walked back to where we had parked the car Monica received a phone call. She motioned for me to come closer and we tried to move away from the swarming tourists. I couldn't make out if she was getting positive or negative news and the suspense was killing me.

'The woman at the CITES office says we can collect the permits this afternoon,' Monica told me, 'but now there is another problem.' She spoke into the phone again, said something in Italian and hung up. 'I'll call her back. She says we can get the permits, but the minister of the environment is angry because he wasn't told about the relocation of the chimp and he wants to postpone it for one week.'

I felt like yelling with frustration. This was like being on a rollercoaster ride and knowing that one wheel was sure to come off and derail you.

'This is insane! What the hell has the minister got to do with anything?'

'His party is very – how would you say it? – very green, and he wants to use the opportunity for publicity.'

'Jackass!' I bellowed.

I needed a miracle. Then, in a moment of sudden clarity the solution came to me. We would smuggle Cozy out of the country. Actually, it wasn't so much smuggling – it was more of a diversion that I had in mind. The laws of the European Union allowed us to drive Cozy to pretty much any other country in Europe. If I could persuade GK Air in Frankfurt to work their magic and get the permits at their end, it *could* be possible. A long shot, maybe, but possible.

'Call her back, Monica,' I said, 'and please emphasise the urgency of our getting Cozy out. Sell it as best you can. Tell them if they don't look the other way Cozy won't be leaving Italy and it will turn into a PR nightmare for them and the minister. If that doesn't work, try the compassion angle. Cozy needs expert attention soon or he will die ...'

We walked into a quiet back street away from the noisy bustle of tourists.

'What is your plan?' she asked.

'I'm not quite sure yet, but tell her that we will drive Cozy to Germany and take a flight from there to Johannesburg. She just needs to make sure that the permits will allow us to do that. I'll figure out all the rest as we go along.'

'Okay,' she said with determination. 'I'll do it.'

She rang the official and started selling her our proposal and sell it she certainly did for by the time she hung up the good news was in.

'She says it's possible. They will meet us in Ancona with the permits.'

'Now you're talking!' I whooped with delight. 'I'm not sure if we are going to pull this off, but ... you're the man ... *girl*, I mean!' I gave her a big hug.

I phoned GK Air and asked them to change the flight from Rome to Frankfurt and to arrange for a truck to drive me and the chimp from Ancona to Frankfurt. It was a lot to ask, and at very short notice. I'm sure if I'd been dealing with any other company I'd have been told to bugger off. Phillip had told me about their efficiency and excellent service when he'd had to move a gorilla from Frankfurt to the Johannesburg Zoo.

Kay, the person I dealt with at GK, sounded like a dynamic young executive.

'It's no problem. We will send a driver to pick you up. Permits are not a problem if you can fax the CITES documentation to us. The flight will be on South African Airways; we have a good relationship with them.'

'And the timing?'

'We'll send the driver tonight. It will take him about eighteen hours to get to Ancona.'

'So that means he'll be there tomorrow afternoon?'

'Ja.'

'I could kiss you, Kay!'

'Not necessary,' he answered drily.

'We're in business,' I told Monica.

But of course we weren't out of the woods yet. There were still a million things that could go wrong on the road to Frankfurt. The time line was close to impossible. The truck was due to arrive in Ancona on the Friday afternoon and we'd have to leave immediately to complete the eighteen-hour return journey to Frankfurt to be in time for the flight to South Africa on the Sunday. The likelihood of all these tight arrangements going according to plan was remote, but I had to try. I phoned Phillip with an update. It was imperative that he saw to the details on his side, including notifying our import agents, arranging truck transport and, last but not least, the state veterinarian and a Parks Board representative who were needed to oversee the quarantine process.

Early the next morning Monica and I left for Ancona, stopping only at a supermarket to buy food supplies for Cozy. It was going to be a long trip to Frankfurt and there'd be no time to stop for supplies. I reckoned that two dozen bananas, half a dozen applies and eight litres of water should be enough for a growing chimp.

On the way Monica filled me in on some of Cozy's details – where he was born, how he came to be in Ancona and the challenges Svetlana had faced taking care of him after his owner died. Cozy had, in fact, been born in the USA. A park in Colorado had a chimpanzee breeding programme and sold the animals to anyone who had enough money –

they were very expensive. It was mostly the entertainment industry that was interested in acquiring chimps and they had become highly sought after. Cozy was no different. His Israeli-born owner was a sort of gypsy with a travelling road show who moved from town to town using Cozy to draw the crowds; they could take photographs with him or buy postcards of him dressed in cute human clothing. But this all came to an end when the owner suffered a fatal heart attack, leaving his girlfriend Svetlana stranded in Italy and having to take care of Cozy.

Apparently the owner's vehicles remained in Ancona, where he had died, and Svetlana found work as a bar tender in a local strip club. With a limited income, a chimpanzee to look after and two trailers to call home, Svetlana did not have an easy time of it, yet it was three years before her cry for help. Cozy lived in the trailer for a total of six years, during the last three of which he never saw the sun and had no contact with anyone other than Svetlana. This was because his display behaviour became very aggressive and the mere sight of people set him off. Svetlana had covered up the windows of the trailer, leaving him in near isolation from the outside world. It was a very sad story.

I couldn't imagine the horror of being kept in a cage in a sunless world for three years. Logic would suggest that if you are unable to take proper care of an animal, you find someone who can. Why did Svetlana wait for such a long time before calling for help? Surely a reasonable human being would never consider locking another up for such a long time and denying him even the touch of sunlight on his skin? I just couldn't understand this and hoped that when I met Svetlana I'd get some answers.

After a few hours of driving through the beautiful Italian countryside we were there – the two trailers instantly identifiable close to the main road on the outskirts of Ancona. They were a Mercedes recreational vehicle and a trailer home parked behind it, the one-time travelling circus. Monica parked her car and we walked up to the trailers. Anxious not to open the wrong door by mistake, we knocked on both doors until a voice called out in Italian.

A fine-featured blonde woman came out of the trailer home and greeted us. 'This is Svetlana,' said Monica as she introduced me.

I guessed that Svetlana was in her late twenties or early thirties. She was strikingly good looking and it was hard to believe that such a lady would be living in a trailer alongside a main road. Svetlana didn't speak a word of English and she and Monica talked Italian to each other. She courteously invited us to join her for a cold drink at the strip club which was closed during the daytime. Even though there was no one there, I felt strangely uncomfortable entering the place and sitting at the bar with the two women.

Svetlana organised soft drinks for us and then embarked on a lengthy conversation with Monica. Feeling once more like a wall painting, not able to understand a word of it, my thoughts turned to the chimp concealed in his trailer. What did he look like? Was he hideous and deformed? Was he going to be so aggressive that I'd be risking my life just entering his domain?

Monica turned to me. 'Svetlana tells me she is very sorry Cozy has to leave. She loves him very much and spends a lot of time with him.'

I nodded. 'I can understand that.'

'She had to cover the windows of his trailer because he went crazy when men walked past. It was the only way to control him.'

'That's a pity. What does he do all day?'

Monica referred the question to Svetlana and then translated her answer. 'She says that she gave him a lot of toys, he has a television on during the day and enjoys that, and she spends time with him when she is not working.'

'Can we go and meet him?' I asked.

Svetlana understood this and immediately got up and ushered us towards the door. As we approached the Mercedes RV Svetlana started talking again, and again Monica translated.

'She used to be a juggler as part of the road show, but when her boyfriend developed chest pains they pulled off here on the side of the road, and she's been here ever since.'

'Damn, that's sad,' I said contemplating the reality of such a hopeless situation.

'She also says that Cozy hates men and that it would be a problem for you to go into his trailer,' Monica continued.

'Can I try?' I asked. 'I have a few tricks up my sleeve.'

After Monica had translated, Svetlana beckoned to me to accompany her. She was smiling, probably thinking that Cozy would go nuts at the sight of me.

Svetlana entered first and there was a loud chimp greeting. The call was unusual and the volume didn't sound as though it came from an emaciated chimpanzee. As if knowing that there would be consequences if she didn't respond immediately, Svetlana walked up to the cage and knelt down beside it.

Hesitant about entering when I didn't quite know what was awaiting me, I paused with one foot on the doorstep and leaned forward to get a better view of the interior. With the windows blocking out the sunlight and no direct lighting above Cozy, I could only make out a shadowy figure at the far end of the RV. I would have to get inside if I wanted to see anything properly. But before I did I uttered a 'pant-hoot' greeting – one of the most studied chimpanzee vocalisations. Cozy erupted from behind the bars making a vocalisation that indicated his fear and uncertainty about what was coming into the trailer. As I entered I had to wait for my eyes to adjust to the dark interior. Behind the stainless steel bars was a four-foot chimp who was as pale as death itself. He was wearing a pair of blue denim shorts that were obviously meant for a child and his waist was shrunken and deformed.

As I approached he quietened down to the point where he was hardly vocalising at all. Svetlana talked to him in Italian, reassuring him in a very calm voice. I hunched down next to Svetlana, careful not to make any sudden movements, and started making recognisable chimp sounds: '*Arg arg arg.*'

Cozy started to exhibit typical chimp socialisation behaviour towards me in what I describe as 'spitballing', rolling his tongue in and out of his mouth, and reaching through the bars in an attempt to groom me. I hesitated, then carefully extended my arm after repositioning my feet to ensure that I would be able to lever myself away from the cage if he tried to grab me. The frail chimp on the other side of the bars didn't look dangerous, but his teeth were something else. To be honest, I think they were in better condition than mine.

Svetlana, clearly blown away by Cozy's reaction to me, shook her head in disbelief. She whispered something to Monica who was standing in the doorway.

'She says she can't believe how nice Cozy is being to you,' Monica translated. 'He usually goes crazy at the sight of men.'

'He's not bad,' I said in a calm tone. 'You just want out, right, my boy?'

'*Arggh*,' was the response.

I knew nothing about Cozy then but over time I would learn that he was an incredibly talkative chimp who enjoyed communicating and would respond each time you engaged with him.

Cozy got up and started to shuffle around his cage which was no larger than six feet square, barely offering freedom of movement and certainly no opportunity to walk around. He grabbed some of his toys and threw them playfully into the air, shaking his head with enjoyment when they hit the ground. What was upsetting me was his deformed waist and I could not for the life of me understand why he was still wearing clothes or why the clothes were so small. At almost ten years old he should have been a lot bigger and stronger, the lack of muscle mass was only too obvious. He didn't strike me as a dangerous chimp at all, just a lonely and frustrated young fellow who was angry at the world for keeping him locked up. Why was he still so nice to Svetlana? The only answer that made sense was that she was the centre of his world, always kind to him, and he could not realise that she was responsible for his worsening condition.

Svetlana was very trusting of Cozy, extending her arm into the cage to rub his back. Did she realise what he could do to her, even in his emaciated state?

It was after 1pm when the CITES officials arrived. The sound of the vehicles induced an aggressive display in Cozy and I thought I should take my leave of him. I went to intercept the officials, trying to explain that Cozy was highly agitated and that it would probably be best if they didn't go into the trailer. Their English was as bad as my Italian and Monica was once again called on to translate.

They didn't seem perturbed about this and gathered together under a tree to wait for events to unfold. Monica approached the female official and asked her about the permits. Then she came towards me.

'They are waiting to hear from a senior official if they can allow us to leave with Cozy,' she said, somewhat concerned.

A feeling of numbness came over me as thoughts of failure once again entered my mind.

'But I thought it was all good to go?' I said.

'It was, but they are still worried about the minister. They are unclear what his intentions are and what repercussions might follow if they let you go. They are waiting for input from the senior official who will phone them later.'

'Do they have the paperwork?'

'Yes.'

The female official came up to us and said in her broken English, 'We go for lunch?'

I felt more like throwing up than eating but for PR reasons I agreed. 'Yes, no problem.'

'I know a place,' she said with a smile.

The cheerful bunch of male officials, five in all, made their way towards their cars. We followed them down the road and pulled into the parking lot of an attractive-looking restaurant. We were ushered inside the restaurant and settled down at a large table. The officials seemed to be enjoying themselves and I had to remind myself that the success of the mission was of no interest or concern to them. It was all my problem and I was finding it difficult to smile and nod my way through the meal.

There was no word from the 'senior' official and at about 4pm we made our way back to the trailers. The veterinarian was already there and had set up a table under the tree. The officials gathered there with him. I decided that I couldn't take any more of this; I needed to know what was going to happen. I gently took the female official's arm and led her to one side.

'Ma'am,' I said, 'I hope you can understand me. I need to ask you really nicely to let us go when the truck arrives. Look the other way, if you have to. Make me a criminal, I really don't care. Just please let us do our job or Cozy will never see the outside of that trailer. I'm sure you don't want to be responsible for that. I know the minister is giving you problems, but if we leave from Frankfurt he won't be able to do anything about it.'

She understood the essence of what I was saying and, looking me straight in the eye, she thought about it for a few seconds.

'Okay.'

I wasn't sure if she was agreeing to take the blame or agreeing to set Interpol on me but at that point the 'okay' was good enough for me.

Just then the blue Peugeot panel van arrived from Frankfurt. I had envisaged something with an open loading bay with chicken cages on the back, Cozy and me bouncing up and down as we escaped to Frankfurt. This was far better, and it was probably capable of keeping up with the speed limit, or even exceeding it.

I approached the truck driver and introduced myself, relieved to find that he spoke a bit of English. I noticed that there was a second person in the vehicle and hoped it was his relief driver and not merely a female companion.

'I'm Eugene,' I said. 'I hope you are ready to leave as soon as we have the chimp loaded in the back?'

'Are you ready to leave already? Okay, no problem. My wife will help with the driving. My name is Hans.'

Hans was a dark-haired German who looked comfortable behind the steering wheel of his van. He also looked as though he had been on the road too long, but there was no need for me to point this out.

'I hope you remembered the crate.'

'No need. The chimp can drive in front with me!'

'Wow – a German with a sense of humour!'

'Ha!'

It was going to be a long journey to Frankfurt and I was relieved that it wasn't going to be in the company of a driver who would depress the hell out of me. I opened the back door and took time to inspect the crate. It was about four and a half feet high and didn't exactly inspire confidence. It was made of six panels of one-inch compressed wood with the side panels having thin steel bars set into them spaced about two inches apart. It had two doors, the first a frame with steel bars that slid into place from above, much the same as our crates at the sanctuary, and the second door was less than an inch thick and fixed with a hinge. My worry was that if Cozy wanted to be difficult he could fit his hand through the steel door and, with enough pressure, break open the outer wooden door. He wouldn't be able to escape, but a yard-long chimp arm extending from the crate, intent on mischief, would be disconcerting to say the least.

I left Hans and went to join the veterinarian who was engaged in a lively conversation with some of the CITES officials.

'Can we get started, doc?' I asked. 'We need to hit the road as soon as possible.'

'Okay,' he said and walked over to the table he had set up under the tree.

'What's the plan?'

'I have prepared the dart,' he said.

'I take it you have darted him a few times,' I said, hoping he knew what he was doing.

'Only twice before, to check on his health, but it should be fine.'

Feeling better knowing about the vet's experience, I stood back as he loaded his dart gun and made his way inside the RV. He had barely made his way in before a hellish scream erupted from the RV. The vet, startled, lost his footing and pulled the trigger prematurely. He didn't bother to look for the dart but was eager to leave the trailer, probably realising that his shot had missed its mark.

Svetlana rushed into the trailer and the screaming stopped. A few seconds later she appeared with the dart in her hand.

Surprised both at her being able to get the dart from Cozy and her bravery in doing so without hesitation, I took the dart from her.

'Thank you.'

She simply nodded, giving me an awkward smile. I think she was overwhelmed by the presence of so many people and that she didn't want to make any suggestions because there were so many wildlife authorities and 'experts' there to deal with things. But she had lived with Cozy for nine and a half years and I was willing to bet my right arm that she knew better than any of us what would work to get Cozy darted.

'I missed,' the veterinarian said apologetically.

'No shit!' I whispered to myself.

Then I asked, louder this time, 'What are we going to do now?' I hoped he had a back-up plan.

'I will make up another dart.'

'Um, sorry, but do you mind if we try something else?'

'What do you have in mind?'

'Why don't we get Svetlana to inject him?'

He hesitated. 'Won't that be dangerous?'

'Well,' I said with a shrug, 'she managed to get the first dart from him, so perhaps he will allow her to inject him.'

Svetlana wasn't taking any of this well. She was standing next to the trailer door and I could see that she desperately wanted to go inside and comfort Cozy. The vet went up to her and asked her if she thought she could inject Cozy.

'Si,' she nodded, looking keen to try something other than darting. The doctor removed the drug from the dart and transferred it to a syringe.

Svetlana calmly took the syringe and went back into the trailer.

I expected this would take her some time, perhaps getting Cozy to turn his back for a scratch and then using the opportunity to inject the contents of the syringe. To everyone's surprise, she emerged from the RV in less than two minutes and handed the empty syringe to the vet. She said she had called Cozy and he had given her his hand and she was able to inject him in the arm.

'Now we wait,' the vet said. 'It should not take more than ten minutes for the Zolital to take effect.'

He was right. In no time at all Cozy was snoring. The veterinarian and I went into the trailer and made our way to the door of the cage. This was the scary part; once we opened the door there would be nothing between us and a chimpanzee that allegedly hated men. Once again my imagination was at work and I could see the newspaper headline: *Chimpanzee on the loose in the Italian countryside.* I swallowed hard as we removed the lock from the cage door.

'Wait … take this to make sure he is sleeping,' the veterinarian said handing me a broom he had found next to the cage.

I took the broom from him imagining how silly I must look holding the broom out in front of me. I had to manoeuvre myself into the back of the cage to make space for the veterinarian at the door; he would have to help me to pick Cozy up as there wasn't enough space to stand upright. The chimp looked as though he weighed no more than sixty pounds. As I stepped over the unconscious Cozy I found myself in an awkward hunched up position. I kept my eyes on his face, watching for any flicker of movement. I had to clear about a yard to get over him and so I took an unusually large step over his body. As soon as my foot came down it gave way under a sponge-like substance I had failed to notice. With no time to check my footing I tumbled forward on to Cozy, my face pressed up against his. I tried to regain my balance, grabbing frantically at the bars on either side of the cage. I recovered eventually and squatted on my haunches, ego bruised and shaken.

I looked at the veterinarian who seemed every bit as shaken as I was. And it was only then that I realised that I had stepped on to a piece of excrement. I had been told that Cozy used to clean up after himself. He'd missed a spot.

'Shit happens,' I said, managing a weak smile.

The vet grabbed Cozy's feet and I took his hands and together we manoeuvred him out of the cage and on to a waiting blanket.

'One more thing that can't wait … will you hand me your scissors?'

The vet looked over his shoulder but it wasn't necessary to repeat the request. Monica ran to retrieve the scissors that were lying on the prepping table. I had tried to loosen the buttons on the pair of denim shorts that seemed to be glued to Cozy as though they were actually growing on him. I had plucked at the trouser legs but there was no way the shorts were coming off. So, scissors in hand, I began to cut away the shorts, starting at the bottom of the trousers on each leg and cutting all the way up to the waist.

Cozy's body looked as though it had been assembled from the spare parts of different chimps. His upper body looked like that of an eight-year-old juvenile while his waist looked like that of a three-year-old. My suspicion was that his waist had become deformed from wearing the tiny pair of shorts for so much of his life. With the shorts removed we set off for the travelling crate which was still in the back of the panel van.

As we left the trailer the officials rushed forward, eager to assist us in carrying Cozy to the crate. Before I slid the steel door closed Svetlana asked if she could put Cozy's favourite toy in with him. It was a yellow plastic duck, reminiscent of a child's bath time toy, worn out and looking as though it had gone a few rounds with – well – an adult chimpanzee. I didn't see any reason to object and let Svetlana enter the cage. She placed the toy next to Cozy and then, overcome with emotion, she started sobbing uncontrollably, stroking his face and whispering words I didn't understand. It was an incredibly sad moment and I found myself having to look away to blink back the tears that were forming in my eyes. Only then did it occur to me that for her this was like giving up a child. I put my hand on her shoulder, wanting to comfort her. She pulled back then and I closed the steel door.

The outer wooden door had a small mesh-covered window. The doors weren't locked so that the vet would be able to act quickly if Cozy experienced complications from the anaesthetic. Svetlana sat in front of the window sobbing. After about twenty minutes Cozy lifted his head and looked up at us peering at him through the mesh. He looked dazed and confused, the lingering after effects of the anaesthetic. He slowly studied his new environment, not recognising any of it. Suddenly he jumped up and moved to the only thing that seemed familiar: Svetlana. He pressed his lips against the mesh, vocalising continuously. There was no doubt in my mind that Cozy was panicking; the cage was unfamiliar in every way and the person who had fed and cared for him was now on the other side of a mesh window.

It was a heart-breaking moment. All my preconceived notions of Svetlana being a bad person disappeared. She may have been ignorant of the fact that Cozy was an animal with highly specific needs but she loved him dearly and it pained me to be the person to take him from her.

Svetlana had her hand against the mesh and with tears running down her cheeks she kissed the mesh and said goodbye.

She got up and said something to Monica, who was now also crying. I was surrounded by sobbing women and I knew this was not a good situation to be caught up in. Any minute now I'd lose all tough guy credibility by crying like a baby myself.

'I'll take good care of him,' I said to Svetlana, my hand on her shoulder.

'She says you must phone as soon as you land in South Africa,' Monica told me.

'Please tell her that I will and that I know he will be happy to be with a lot of hairy friends at the sanctuary.'

I gave both the weeping women a hug and walked over to the officials to collect my paperwork. Italians don't mind showing their emotions and all the officials, both male and female, were sniffing or choking one way and another. There was no hesitation in handing over the documentation, and the female official even mustered a 'good luck'.

Hans reluctantly closed the doors with me in the back. It was quite surreal sitting in the dark with Cozy and it took some minutes to sink in that I had managed to beat the odds and was on my way to Frankfurt with Cozy. We were a long way from the border, and an even longer way from Frankfurt but there was no sound from Cozy as we started our eighteen-hour journey. I took some clothing out of my bag and made myself a cushion to rest my head on. If Cozy was going to sleep off the drugs then I might as well also use the opportunity to get some rest.

The first few hours were uneventful but the temperature was still high at around 8pm and I was worried that Cozy might be getting dehydrated. I hoped that he would drink from the bottle but this would be the first contact I would have with him since leaving Ancona.

I opened a bottle of mineral water and positioned myself against the mesh.

'Hey, boy ...' I was cut short by a loud scream – it seemed as though this was the first time Cozy had realised there was someone in the back of the van with him. The effects of the anaesthesia had clearly worn off and he was going to make himself heard. He continued screaming and waving his hand at me in a very human way, as if to say 'Buzz off!'

I didn't want to stress him further, so I backed off. His loud screaming in the confined space was almost unbearable.

'Enough already!' I yelled back at him, but I doubt that he heard me above his screams.

Eventually he quietened and settled down again.

I couldn't sleep, so I passed the time reading a Clive Cussler novel that I'd brought with me from South Africa. The light from my headlamp disturbed Cozy, but not for long. After driving for about two hours I started to worry. Cozy had not drunk or eaten anything since we left Ancona. I had to do something, so I cut up a banana and an apple which I pushed through the mesh of the wooden door. Cozy, unimpressed, began to scream again. It was dark in the crate so I couldn't see him thrashing about but when he started beating the bars I got the message. He was not interested in the fruit at all. I had to try and give him some water, so I braced myself against his screams and slowly poured some water through the mesh. He wasn't interested in that either and his violent behaviour just intensified.

Cozy had warmed to me when he was in his own cage in the trailer but now that he was in a strange cage and separated from Svetlana he wasn't happy at all.

We made one stop before leaving Italy and Hans let me know when we'd crossed the border into Austria. The Schengen agreement signed by twenty-five European countries allowed for easy access across borders. The 800 miles still to go were the least of my worries. The temperature began to drop dramatically and sometime after midnight it had become uncomfortably chilly. I knocked on the panel that separated the driver's cabin from the back and Hans answered.

'Ja?'

'Where are we?'

'We are driving through the Alps.'

'Really? Do you mind if I sit in front for a while?'

'I thought you were never going to ask!' Hans chuckled as he slowed the vehicle down.

I was glad of the chance to stretch my legs, but what really made an impact on me was the amazing view. It was just a few days short of full moon and the snowy mountain peaks that surrounded us gleamed in the moonlight.

'Damn, it's cold!' I said, rubbing my arms to get my circulation moving.

'Yes,' said Hans. 'We are quite high.' I hoped he was referring to the altitude and not to his mental state.

'Are you doing all right with the back-to-back eighteen-hour journey?' I asked studying his eyes for signs of fatigue.

'Ja! Just another day at the office for me. Let's go now!'

His wife shuffled to the middle of the front seat to make space for me. I stared out of the window, captivated by the beautiful view of mountains and dense forests.

'Wow, I wish I could walk through those forests,' I said. 'The wildlife must be wonderful.'

'What wildlife?' Hans replied. 'There is nothing left here.'

'You're kidding, right?'

'No, there is nothing. Everything was hunted a long time ago.'

I thought about this, actually not wanting to contemplate the idea of beautiful forests being empty of the creatures that justified their existence. I read later that more than half of Europe's animal species are facing extinction. Ongoing development and population growth in Europe after the 1500s led to a dramatic increase in animal extinction. Species such as wolves and bison that once roamed the forests were lost by no later than 1920. Having grown up with wild animals grazing on our lawn an everyday sight, this was a fact I found difficult to grasp. Even though South Africa is considered a country undergoing rapid development relative to other African countries, I had never felt that human encroachment was destroying our connection with our environment. I realised that my isolation growing up on a game reserve in Africa had made me ignorant of much that had happened and was still happening elsewhere.

Was the human race really responsible for the emptiness of these beautiful forests? Preoccupied with these thoughts, I briefly forgot about my problems with Cozy. I knew that I still had a lot to learn about the state of our planet. My travels, and the special people I met on them, opened my eyes to the challenges our environment was facing, and to some degree this changed my perspective on the human race. One doesn't have to be a genius to realise that we as a species are the problem and that something drastic needs to happen before the zebras grazing my lawn are no longer an everyday sight for my children, and their children. What could I do about it? I didn't have the solution. I was just a guy who rescued animals in need. Maybe the solution was as simple as that. If every human being took the time to save just a single animal things could be different.

After some time Hans decided that he couldn't go any further. He needed to pull over and take a rest. I was happy to rejoin Cozy who seemed calm, only uttering a single '*urg urg*' when I climbed into the back. I had not been expecting to be exposed to the freezing night temperature of the Alps and did not have a jersey or jacket with me. All I could do was put on as many shirts as possible and avoid contact with anything metallic that would chill me to the marrow. Right about then the blanket I had left with Cozy started to seem attractive. Poor Cozy – if I was feeling the cold so much, what sort of time was he having? I shuffled up to the mesh and peered into the cage and switched on the headlamp to search for the poor chap. I didn't expect the sight that met my eyes. Cozy was lying on his back, the blanket wrapped around him, playing with the fold-over piece as if he was more bored than cold. He looked at me and I swear he was taunting me, rolling around in his blanket and making playful sounds.

'Yeah, laugh it up, fuzzball,' I said with a chuckle.

'*Urrgghh*,' was his brief reply.

I huddled up against my bag and settled in for what was to be a very cold four-hour rest.

Hans started up the van again at about 4am and we continued on our journey.

At breakfast time I knew I had to face Cozy and make another attempt to get him fed and hydrated. Again, I cut up a banana and an apple and moved towards the mesh of the crate. This time I was planning to open the outer wooden door and feed him through the bars rather than squashing the fruit through the small openings in the mesh. There were two serious risks to take account of: first, there was no lock on the inner sliding door and once the outer door was open there was nothing to stop Cozy lifting the sliding door; second, there was the risk that he would grab me through the bars and even though he was so emaciated he could be a threat if he panicked. But I figured the risk was worth it. Cozy desperately needed something in his stomach, especially if we had another hot day ahead of us.

I slowly unlocked the wooden door and peered through the bars. Cozy was wise to what I was doing and gave his usual earth-shattering scream. I cringed as the sound pierced my eardrums. This wasn't going to be easy! I persevered, trying to ignore his outburst and moved cautiously up to the bars, ready to jump back if he lunged at me.

Eventually, I could take no more of his screaming. *'URGGGGGHHH!'* I screamed back at him. He immediately quietened down and looked at me in confusion, as if he was not quite sure what had just happened.

There were a few uncomfortable seconds of silence.

'Eat! *Now!'* I barked, shoving a handful of fruit through the bars. He did not hesitate for a moment. Shuffling up to the bars he slowly brought his mouth up to my hand, his eyes never leaving my face. I maintained my angry facial expression. Only afterwards did I realise that I had portrayed an image of dominance and Cozy had accepted it. Once the first piece of banana was in his mouth he started to vocalise in delight, eagerly taking more fruit from my hand.

I had broken through Cozy's defences and at that moment an unshakeable friendship was born. He was certainly not a chimp who warmed to just anyone. I was the first human male who had had contact with him for years, which had resulted in his going crazy at the mere sight of one, yet this was the moment it all changed for him. And for me. I didn't know then that Cozy would become my window into the world of chimpanzees, teaching me that friendship really was possible between different species. Sure, I had grown up surrounded by wild animals, but this was different. Cozy was different.

Cozy finished half a dozen bananas and the same number of apples. Then he drank half a bottle of water and he turned his back for a scratch. He was a completely different chimp, showing not a single sign of aggression.

Early on the afternoon of 8 July we reached Frankfurt. We drove straight to the part of the airport where Cozy would be readied for his departure with South African Airways. I had never seen an airport like Frankfurt before. To begin with, it was huge and the special animal holding facilities were amazing – Cozy had his own little room while he waited for his flight. I took a towel from my pack and covered the crate so that there would be no distractions for Cozy.

We had made it and GK Air took care of the rest.

The next few hours were easy as pie. I was feeling the lack of sleep but once on board the plane I slept like a baby. I had Cozy on the plane with me and there was nothing anyone could do to stop me from taking him home.

EIGHT

COMRADE COZY – A NEW LIFE

Our reception at O R Tambo International Airport in Johannesburg was amazing. The entire team had come to meet us – Phillip, Natasha, even my father and brother were there to escort us back to the sanctuary. Now only a four-hour drive stood between Cozy and a new life. He would have to stick it out in quarantine for three months, but that was a small price to pay for what awaited him once he had served his time.

When we reached the sanctuary the state veterinarian cleared our paperwork and we moved Cozy's crate to the cage that would be his home for the quarantine period. In terms of the South African

Veterinary Service regulations only a handful of people were allowed to enter the building. Natasha had assumed the responsibility of quarantine manager and I couldn't think of a better person for the job as she was so incredibly caring towards any animal in need. The added advantage, of course, was that she was female and would be the preferred 'go to' for any infant chimpanzee that might have to spend time in quarantine.

Mindful of the episode with Amadeus, we didn't take any chances and secured the crate to the quarantine cage with ratchet-tightening ropes. I untied the piece of string that I had carried around my leg for the entire mission and used it to secure the cage door just in case Cozy decided to pull the same stunt as Amadeus. But there was no threat from Cozy – quite the opposite. As he got out of the crate and came into view the full extent of his emaciation became apparent. He was skin and bone.

The sight of his deformed body was almost too much to bear. One thing was clear; if Cozy was going to become a normal chimp again he was going to need a lot of help to get well. It was already dark by the time we left the quarantine building. Family and friends were braving the cold – but at around 14°C it was far warmer than the Alps. I was overjoyed to be back with my family, especially Natasha. If I'm away from her for more than a day I really start missing her!

The prospect of spending more time at home was, however, not looking too good. Phillip told me that I might have to leave again almost immediately for Angola as he had received word that Sally's permit had been approved. But this wasn't the only exciting development; several other missions had popped up unexpectedly and were as important as Sally's pending relocation. The next few weeks would see an intense effort to rescue and relocate not only Sally but also two other chimpanzees. The others that made it were Joao, the fifty-two-year-old male from Mozambique and the fifteen-month infant from the United Arab Emirates. Each one of them would turn out to be incredibly special with vastly different personalities.

The back-to-back missions were by no means easy. But each one provided me with more experience at dealing with the unexpected problems that seemed inevitable.

At the end of July we had four chimpanzees of all shapes and sizes in quarantine. Sally, who was cute and mostly quiet, was placed on the same side of the corridor as Cozy. We were especially jubilant about her arrival. After my earlier tearful departure from her, and my fear that I would never see her again, it was wonderful to have her with us at last. Up until then Sally had never spent time with another chimpanzee and we were intrigued to see how she would react during the introductions.

Zeena was the other infant chimpanzee. She was estimated to be about the same age as Sally, but she was shaved from head to toe and resembled nothing so much as a bird whose feathers had been plucked. Our part in her rescue was limited to the logistical arrangements in having her transferred to the sanctuary from Dubai. She arrived in a small wooden crate and once out of it she proved both aggressive and mistrustful, lashing out at anyone or anything that came too close to her. She had clearly been abused and the veterinarian who had rescued her confirmed that she had been subjected to the strange practice of being shaved, evidently for purposes of hygiene. It was easy to understand her anger and only time would tell if good treatment would make her warm up to human beings.

Apart from Cozy, Joao was the only other adult in quarantine. He was a big, muscular chimp who must have weighed around 145 pounds. He had been abandoned by his previous owner, a man who owned a circus and whose legacy of animal abuse lives on through his descendants who still own and operate circuses in South Africa. A circus was in fact the very first place where I saw a chimpanzee. I was no more than four years old and would not have understood then that circuses rely on the enslavement of wild and exotic animals for purposes of 'entertaining' the public.

Joao was left at the Maputo Zoo as an infant and had one companion for five years before that individual died of unknown causes. He survived the seventeen-year conflict in Mozambique, living on the bare minimum – food provided by a few caring individuals. Bald, and with most of his teeth gone, he had at least filled out in bulk after the war when the Zoo Association found the means to take better care of the animals at the zoo. A few South African organisations had tried to relocate him at different times, but without success. With careful timing, luck and a good argument I convinced Joao's main caretaker, Helena Nicolau, to support his move to Chimp Eden and I was ecstatic when I heard of the association's belated decision to agree to the move. The first time I laid eyes on Joao his coat was puffed up, probably because he was excited for some or other reason. The hair of his thick coat was so long that when he was puffed up he looked twice as big – hence the source of the rumour I started that he was a two hundred pound chimpanzee.

The logistics involved in moving Joao were relatively simple and involved crossing the border between Mozambique and South Africa by truck and a distance of only about 125 miles. We knew very little about Joao's personality, but were aware that visitors to the zoo often gave him alcohol and cigarettes for their own amusement. Now he was part of a new family and we had to figure out which was the best group match for his introduction. We placed him out of sight of the other chimps in quarantine simply because we were afraid of how the two adult males might react when they saw each other for the first time. Phillip thought that vocalisation between him and Cozy might be the best way to start.

Of the four chimpanzees in quarantine Cozy was the saddest case. It was evident from the start that his development would be slow. If I really did believe that wishes came true, when I flipped that coin into Trevi Fountain I'd probably have wished that his rehabilitation would be as easy as giving him a spacious wild enclosure that he would take to like a duck to water. I hadn't spent any time with Cozy in the first weeks after his arrival because of the other rescue work that had to be done but once I was back and the other three chimps had joined him in quarantine they all became the centre of my world.

The first time Cozy saw me again he was beside himself with joy. I'd like to think that our race to freedom and subsequent screaming match in the back of the panel van had something to do with it – to such a degree that he now regarded me as his best friend. One could also reason that he was more interested in me than anyone else because I was the person who saw him through from the small confines of his cage in the RV to the roomy environment of the quarantine cage. Whatever the reason, Cozy was eager to have contact with me and I spent hours sitting next to his cage scratching his back and watching him prance around. He had changed little in the four weeks that I'd been away and still looked incredibly uncomfortable when walking, rather like the poor coordination of a newborn or the awkward movement of an eighty-year-old.

Dr Stephen van der Spuy, the director of the Johannesburg Zoo and a highly experienced vet who frequently assisted us with rescue operations, had commented that Cozy would most likely never be a normal chimpanzee because of his lack of muscle development, and that he might even need corrective surgery if there was to be any chance of him living a normal life. Yet to me and to Phillip there had to be a simpler way. Neither of us had answers yet, but one interesting fact about Cozy had come to light during my absence. Phillip had discovered that Cozy had an insatiable appetite for peanut butter!

Peanut butter is a great source of nutrition for development because of its high protein and calorie content. The Aztecs who made a form of peanut butter hundreds of years ago may have had different intentions for it than fattening up a chimpanzee, but it was great news for us because it would help speed up Cozy's recovery.

Now we needed a way of getting him to move around more, especially a way of getting him to climb. I've mentioned that Cozy liked to prance around his cage, but he far more preferred lying on his mattress and having his back scratched. After a bit of scratching myself – head scratching, that is – I came up with a way of getting him to move by placing chunks of peanut butter on the ceiling bars of his cage. He wouldn't only have to climb the side of the cage, which was about eight feet high, but he would also have to move horizontally when he got to the top. It worked brilliantly and had him climbing as often as I could summon up the energy to put the peanut butter in place.

During one of these rehabilitation exercises our friendship was tested to the extreme. Each time I climbed on to the top of the cage I lay down flat on my stomach in order to be close to Cozy when he came swinging in for the peanut butter. On one occasion my rubber boot got jammed in between the small ceiling mesh blocks and I crashed down face first. A Leatherman multi-tool dislodged itself from my pocket and dropped down into the cage beside Cozy. When I came to my senses I noticed, to my horror, that the tool had opened to expose a blade. Panic-stricken, I yelled, 'No, Cozy! Don't touch it!' as I made my way back down to the corridor as quickly as possible.

I lost sight of Cozy as I was climbing down but I could hear him vocalising his normal hoots. When I arrived at the front of his cage I found him standing upright with his back against the wall. With an expression of fear on his face he looked to me to save him from the alien object that had fallen from the unknown into his small world.

'Quick, Cozy, give it to me!' I shouted, pointing towards the tool and edging forward to encourage him.

He moved forward immediately and hesitantly picked up the tool before pushing it through the bars for me to take hold of.

I was no expert in chimp behaviour but I knew that it was uncommon for a chimpanzee to follow orders to such a degree, giving up something as potentially interesting and valuable as a multi-tool.

'Good boy!' I said with a nervous laugh, feeling as though I had dodged a bullet.

'*Hoo hoo hoo aggaahh,*' he answered, a look of pride on his face. He was suddenly relaxed, the tension of the moment gone along with the strange object that had made his friend so nervous. Cozy trusted me, and soon I would have to show him that same trust or risk losing the opportunity to help him join a family.

Things were not progressing as well on the other side of the corridor. Joao, without alcohol or cigarettes for a few days now, was clearly showing withdrawal symptoms. Every time he laid eyes on me or Phillip he lost his marbles, kicking the internal steel hatch door so hard that it made my ears ring. From our first impressions of Joao it didn't seem too promising that he would be able to be integrated with any of the quarantine chimps. Only time would tell whether Joao would accept us as his new caretakers and, more importantly, if he would be able to be integrated with Abu's group.

The weeks passed and Phillip and I spent most of our time working between the construction of the outside enclosures and the rehabilitation work in the quarantine building. So far we had managed to get only Sally and Zeena into the same cage, but as far as I understood introductions between infants was usually no big deal.

The real challenge lay ahead: introducing Cozy to Sally and Zeena. It was Phillip's hope that with only two infants in his environment Cozy would have less threatening circumstances in which to develop.

Cozy did have a few disadvantages. Having grown up with only humans around him, he seemed to have few chimp vocalisations of his own. We were worried that he might not be able to communicate very well and that, in the wrong company, he might be injured or even killed. So Phillip and I made what might have been a controversial decision, one that would either be praised or criticised, depending on your point of view. We wanted to learn more about chimpanzee communication in order to better understand and help chimps like Cozy. He would surely not be the only chimp to come to Chimp Eden that had problems communicating. Perhaps if we could learn to communicate with them we would be better equipped to deal with introducing them to other chimps, not to mention instances where physical rehabilitation would require us to be in the same environment as an adult chimpanzee.

There were several major problems, of which the most obvious was the risk of attack. If a chimp objected to our presence, for whatever reason, a violent attack could ensue and since we humans are not nearly as tough as our hairy cousins there was no question about who would come off worst. The second problem was learning the language. It wasn't as if we could pick up a manual and follow its instructions. Chimpanzee language was complex and researchers had different views on how to interpret it.

I insisted that I be the one to take the risk, at least initially, until we developed confidence in our ability to understand chimp language. For one thing, I was more mobile than Phillip and would be quicker getting in and out of the interleading hatches between adjacent quarantine cages if things started to go wrong. On the other hand Phillip, with his years of experience, had a greater understanding of chimp language as far as vocalisations were concerned and his interpretations would be invaluable.

This was our plan. We would spend days, or weeks if need be, observing Cozy and the other chimps. We wanted to understand each vocalisation and the behaviour pattern that accompanied it. Observation was also key in determining what triggered violent behaviour patterns and whether there were any warning signs of such behaviour. The procedure of going into the cage with Cozy would be much the same as any other chimp introduction we'd overseen. I would have to sit at the cage door, wait for the right invitation signals and if they came the door would open and I would have to deal with whatever came next. The 'whatever came next' was the important part. We needed to know more about it or there would be no science to it and it would be pretty much like leaping into the lion's den with the dinner bell around my neck. We needed to identify vocalisations and behaviour unique to Cozy so that there would be no surprises. It would be like learning different dialects in chimpanzee language.

And so our observations started. I found it hard to focus on Cozy and only Cozy when there was a general cry for attention from the other chimps and hissy-fits being thrown because I wasn't responding. So I started watching Joao and the two youngsters as well and gained insights into a more 'general' language. Phillip and I also did some research to find out as much as we could, taking examples from experts in the field such as Dr Frans de Waal and Dr Jane Goodall. The biggest challenge was matching the observed behaviour of wild chimpanzees with that of captive chimpanzees. Growing up in different environments, especially traumatic ones, can have a significant impact on how chimps communicate and deal with social issues.

We had to start somewhere, so we decided to move ahead with Cozy. I perfected the 'pant-hoot' to a T. I knew how to socialise with general grooming behaviour and knew enough about physical posture to be sure that I wasn't going to threaten him in any way.

The big day arrived. I was as nervous as hell. I put on two jackets for a bit of protection in case he bit me. But in reality this was only to give me a sense of false security because chimp attacks are usually so violent that there is little chance the victim will survive. During my research the past few weeks I had found numerous references to chimp attacks on humans, and also on members of their own species. There was a general pattern to the attack. In the case of a human, the chimpanzee would first ensure that his victim was knocked off his feet, so it would either be a slow, upright approach, or a more direct running approach to hit and kick to maximum effect, ultimately knocking the victim to the ground with incredible force. The next part isn't always the same but generally this was what could be expected. The victim tries to protect himself by warding off the attacker with his arms and hands, so usually fingers and often hands are severed by the attacker with just a few quick biting actions. If the victim attempts to kick while lying on the ground it might motivate the attacker to bite the feet as well.

Next, there could be powerful punches to the chest and head, and biting of the face as well. If you're a male, the chances are good that your genitals will be removed just to seal the argument.

I visualised all these violent scenes as I bent over to scratch Cozy's back. He was such a frail chimpanzee that the chances of him doing any of the above to me were slim. Still, he did have a mean set of teeth and I'd be wise to steer clear of them at all costs. I started to talk to Cozy, as I had done almost every morning for the past few days. He responded in his usual way, but we were looking for a specific behaviour pattern that would indicate he was ready for the next step. We were hoping to see Cozy initiate socialising behaviour, as he had done almost every day with me and then get him to realise that I would be entering his cage to continue socialising. Phillip would then open the hatch door, giving Cozy unrestricted movement around me.

It wasn't long before Cozy reached out a hand and started grooming my arm which I had placed horizontally against the bars. I looked at Phillip for confirmation. 'I don't think it's going to get better than this,' he said, looking pretty confident.

'All right,' I said, taking a deep breath. 'Moment of truth.'

I walked into the cage adjacent to Cozy's. We had earlier moved Sally one cage up in the row of six cages that lined the corridor. A feeling of helplessness came over me. There is a difference between preaching and practising what you preach.

'I have to lock you in,' Phillip said, 'just in case he decides to take a stroll.'

'Of course. So the plan is to open the hatch door a little at a time and see what he does.'

'Yep. The slots in the hatch lever will prevent him from forcing the door open,' Phillip reminded me.

The hatch in the middle of the wall separating two adjacent cages was opened and closed by a lever situated in the corridor. The lever had slots cut into it one inch apart, allowing the operator of the lever to control the amount of space that the door was opened. This had been designed specifically because of its advantages when introducing chimps to each other and it was also a safety mechanism in the event of a chimp trying to force open the hatch when a keeper was cleaning an adjacent cage.

'Okay, ready when you are,' I said going down on my haunches next to the hatch. Phillip opened the hatch door about three inches, allowing me enough space to look through but not enough for Cozy to try and grab me.

'*Argh argh argh,*' I said while peering at him through the opening. Once he realised that the door was opening he immediately walked up to it. I backed up a tad while he explored the opening. He tried to squeeze through but found out soon enough that it wouldn't work. I motioned for him to sit down.

'Sit down, boy. Calm down.'

Cozy obediently sat down at the opening, perfectly calm, and looked me in the eye. I moved closer to the hatch and placed my arm close to it. I pulled up the sleeve of my jacket, exposing my arm. Cozy started spitballing and tried to groom my arm through the opening.

'Don't take your eyes off him,' Phillip warned.

'I won't. Can you open the door another inch?'

'Will he get through?'

'No.'

Phillip lifted the lever and opened the door another inch before dropping the lever into the slot.

Cozy stood up and looked as though he was going to try to squeeze through the opening. Again I motioned for him to sit down and again he obeyed. He continued to groom my arm.

'I think we should go ahead and open ... what do you think?' I asked. I was secretly hoping Phillip would say no, but he'd observed Cozy's calm behaviour and there didn't seem to be cause for alarm.

'Yes, I think we are good to go,' Phillip replied. 'In fact, I think we might be working backwards if we don't go ahead.' His voice was calm enough but his face looked serious.

'Let's rock,' I said, standing upright and moving to the far end of the cage.

I wanted to give myself as much space as possible in case Cozy came through the door and decided to display. We knew that sometimes during 'introductions' male chimps would stand upright, hair erect, and then charge both on all fours and standing upright, beating walls and doors and anything else that was in their way, including the chimp or human being 'introduced' to them. This behaviour is intended to be a display of dominance, and we were worried that Cozy might try to dominate me in this way.

My heart was pounding in my chest and sweat was dripping from my forehead. I don't think I had ever before in my life been as tense as I was at that moment. I would repeat this many times in the future, but that first time was definitely the worst. I knew that there were many gaps in my knowledge and trying to imitate behaviour that you'd read about in books and research reports wasn't the easiest thing in the world. If I inadvertently did something wrong, something that might be interpreted as hostile, or if my body language seemed unreceptive, Cozy's mood could change for the worse which would put me at considerable risk. But I reminded myself that he wasn't big and strong like the chimp across the corridor so I had a pretty good chance of making it out in one piece.

The moment of truth. Phillip opened the hatch all the way and the loud clanking noise it made immediately had Cozy on his feet. He was walking upright and moving towards me faster than I had ever seen him move before. I stood up straight and held my breath, wondering what was coming next. Cozy flung his arms around my waist, ramming his head into my stomach. I was helpless to resist and for a few seconds I wasn't sure what was going on.

'Be careful ... it's okay, it's okay,' Phillip was providing a running commentary on what he was observing.

I cautiously rested my hand on Cozy's head. 'Good boy,' I said. '*Argh argh argh.*'

Fortunately I didn't know that Cozy had his mouth open against my stomach or I might have had a moment of panic. However, this was a behaviour that I would later call an 'open mouth greeting' and it indicates acceptance between two chimps when they first make contact.

I slowly pushed Cozy away from me and knelt down next to him.

'Sit down, boy.'

He eagerly grabbed my arm and pulled back the sleeve. The expression on his face was something like that of a kid in a candy store. Googly-eyed, he started spitballing and grooming my arm furiously. I calmed down a little, but not too much. I was resting on my haunches but ready to jump if need be.

'Careful,' Phillip warned me again.

Cozy locked his eyes on my face as if he was searching for something. What it was I didn't know and I didn't want to think about it too hard. He fixed his eyes on my forehead and let go of my arm. Then he lifted his hand and started to flick his fingers towards my forehead.

'That's weird behaviour,' Phillip said. 'I'm not sure I like it.'

But I didn't want to give up yet so I just let the moment play out. Nothing Cozy had done up to that point had made me feel threatened, although I had to admit the finger flicking was a bit odd. He slowly reached up with both hands, my eyes tracking them as they moved

Saving Chimpanzees

towards my forehead. It was risky – but no risk, no reward. I felt him scratching at a tiny lesion on my skin. He seemed to think it was something that had to be removed with great urgency. I couldn't help but chuckle when I realised what he was doing.

'Ouch! That hurt,' I said, pulling my head back.

He looked me in the eye, opened his mouth and stuck out his tongue. '*Arghh*,' he said. To me it was as if he was saying, 'Oh stop whining, you big baby.' Cozy was just being Cozy.

In all, I spent about ten minutes with Cozy. When I left the separation was as simple as luring Cozy through the hatch and closing it behind him. With a big high-five I joined Phillip in the corridor and we discussed what we had learned from the introduction. In retrospect, Cozy wasn't far off the mark. Normal greeting behaviour in chimpanzees includes hugging as well as the scary open mouth greeting. If anything, *my* behaviour didn't quite match a normal chimp greeting and acceptance. But, later, after many long hours of chimp observation we would have a much better understanding of their language.

My bond with Cozy was firmly cemented. However, the goal was not to get him more used to humans but rather to a group of other chimpanzees. We had to get moving on the introductions. Sally and Zeena did not have a perfect relationship as the two of them did not exactly see eye to eye. They tolerated each other in the same cage and for the time being that was enough to advance to the next level, which was to get Cozy integrated with them. The next few days I focused on strengthening my bond with Cozy, and Phillip also introduced himself, again with a positive outcome.

And so we moved on to the introduction that would see Chimp Eden's first group of rescued chimps come together. Again, the first step was to open the hatch a few inches with Cozy on one side and the reluctant

Sally-Zeena partnership on the other. With the hatch open just a tad both parties could stare at each other and make warning calls. As with my introduction to Cozy, we had to wait until the right signs came from both sides before opening the hatch all the way. It was Cozy who eventually became more receptive to the idea of the introduction. He sat in front of the hatch sucking his thumb and flicking his fingers at the infants next door. The small opening between the cages gave them the opportunity to make friends, but the introduction was not without its challenges.

Zeena revealed herself to us as deeply mistrustful and preferred to be on her own rather than with another chimp. Even after many days spent with Sally, and even sleeping in the same cage with her, she still showed a reluctance to participate in friendly behaviour. There was not even acceptance behaviour towards Sally and Zeena relished every opportunity to bully her by pulling her hair and so on. I'd like to think that she was not aggressive by nature and that earlier abuse was the probable reason for her dysfunctional behaviour. It was clear, however, that she wasn't going to be a pivotal member of the group in terms of teaching us about acceptance behaviour and vocalisations; from her we would learn more about dealing with an unpredictability that could throw a spanner in the works at any time.

After more than a week of the introduction process we reached a point where we felt we were not moving forwards. Sally and Cozy were showing some interest in each other but it was nothing earth shattering. But the important thing was that we did not see any aggressive behaviour from Cozy. If we let too much time pass before full contact with the infants he might become frustrated. So, as a final step, we opened the hatch and Cozy rushed into the next door cage. The two infants had become used to the hatch never being fully opened and were both surprised and overwhelmed. They both shot up the side walls and hung from the ceiling bars with Sally staying as close to us as possible. Cozy was glad to be in the room and his initial approach to the infants was very calm. He stayed on the ground but slowly reached up to both of them with one hand. But there was no positive reaction from the other two. He then walked over to where I was standing at the door and sat down and sucked his thumb.

It was hard to believe that Cozy had once been a violent chimp, displaying and kicking the bars of his cage at the sight of any stranger. He seemed a completely different chimp, bonding with both Phillip and me and trying his best to make friends with other chimps. His signature pose was an upright one with his chest out, while he uttered 'arrghh'. This earned him the nickname 'The Italian Stallion'.

Using my bond with Cozy and Sally we tried the strategy of playing an intermediary role. I went into the cage with the three of them and tried to get the infants to come down from the ceiling. Eventually Sally came down. I groomed Cozy continuously and by offering Sally the same treatment the two of them were eventually in the same space, although they didn't interact much at first. Cozy made attempts but Sally wasn't responsive so whatever interaction took place was with me sitting between them.

At long last the day came when Sally climbed down from the bars and submitted to Cozy, after which she threw her arms around the Italian Stallion in a heart-warming moment. It took months, years even, before Zeena did the same. Cozy and Zeena never really developed a bond between them. I didn't blame Cozy. Zeena rarely displayed true friendship behaviour and always tried to find ways of unbalancing the group. With the three of them now part of a group, which we called the 'infant group', we would soon be able to move them into the second enclosure which was nearing completion.

It made me sad to see Joao sitting all alone in his cage on the opposite side of the corridor. He wouldn't be able to join this group because he was such a big chimp with a scary display and it would be too risky to try to integrate him into the newly formed infant group. Yet there was a softer side to him that emerged when he saw Natasha. She felt sorry for him and he desperately needed a friend. And so a weird bond developed between them. Every time she walked past him he would vocalise and she would respond by giving him either food or drink. Yet there were times when he wanted more personal attention and so Natasha started to give him regular 'manicures'. The two of them would sit together for hours, Joao sticking his fingers through the bars patiently having his hideously long nails filed while Natasha talked to him like an old friend.

After three months of quarantine for the infants, and four for Cozy, we were finally ready for the move to the big enclosure. And we didn't need a grain of anaesthetic either. The strategy we devised, for Zeena first, involved trapping her in a travel crate with special manoeuvring and smart thinking, and the rest was daring but worth the effort. My father drove his Ford F250 pickup truck with enclosed canopy into the quarantine area. Then we proceeded with our plan to move the other two chimps. Phillip and I walked Cozy out of the building, one of us on either side of him (although he was glued to my hand) and Sally perched on Phillip's hip, as we made our way to the back of the pickup that would drive us straight into the new enclosure. Neither chimp made any attempt to leave our sides. To everyone's delight Cozy followed me into the back of the truck with Sally joining him soon after. Phillip closed us in under the canopy of the pickup and my father drove us to the enclosure. I had my hands on Cozy's shoulders, doing my best to keep him calm as he embarked on a series of new experiences. He had not seen the outside world to any significant degree for at least four years and he looked about wildly as we left the quarantine building and drove the short distance to the enclosure. But he never once attempted to leave my side. It was as if he was totally overwhelmed and beyond knowing how to respond.

My heart was beating loudly, adrenalin and emotions suffocating me.

This was a pretty big moment. Cozy had become my friend. I thought that I understood him and knew what he needed to get better. Part of that would be giving him what all wild creatures have a right to: a wild environment and freedom to be with their own kind.

When we reached the enclosure the truck was backed up with the tailgate facing the hatch door that separated the sleeping quarters from the outside enclosure. The hatch was open and Phillip lifted the canopy and dropped the tailgate. I held on to Cozy and also grabbed Sally who by now was looking for some reassurance. With Sally on my hip I jumped down and went through the hatch and put her down. I had to be quick because Cozy was the real risk. If at any time he felt I was abusing his trust he would not hesitate to try and escape. If he managed that he could end up testing the high voltage fences and, given his poor condition, that could be a disastrous encounter.

I called him down: 'Come on, Cozy, *urgh urgh urgh.*'

He was still a weak chimp and was struggling to climb down from the tailgate. So I reached up and grabbed him under the armpits and lowered him to the ground. He followed me into the sleeping quarters. It had all gone very smoothly. The hatch was closed but the chimps had a big room to move about in. It didn't take long to get Zeena freed into the adjacent introduction room. This time she was happy to move across her room to join her comrades on the opposite side of the interleading hatch.

I have to admit that this was a very emotional experience for me. Just a few short months ago no one apart from Svetlana would have dared to come into contact with Cozy, and then only through the steel bars of a cage. He was an outcast, regarded as a dangerous animal who had to be kept isolated in a secure steel cage. He was not allowed to see the outside world for fear that he would scare everyone with his violent displays and wild screaming. Now he was interacting with his human caretakers, showing complete trust in them. In particular, I think it was the trust that he had bestowed on me that moved me most.

The jubilant Chimp Eden team welcomed the new arrivals, now able to see their faces for the first time.

With Cozy seeming to be cooperative and trusting, the only wild card we had to worry about was Zeena and her release into the outside enclosure. With her disregard for her human keepers and apparently no need for reassurance from them, we never knew what to expect from her. The next day would be tricky. We planned to control the release of the three chimps so that we could deal with each one's reactions individually.

Apart from the main room, the sleeping quarters had two introduction rooms with interleading hatches and we decided to separate Sally from Cozy and take her out first. All went according to plan and as I left the sleeping quarters with Sally on my hip Phillip joined us and we both took her for a twenty-minute stroll through the enclosure. She was happy to leave my side and darted up and down trees. As soon as we moved away from her she immediately ran back to either Phillip or me. Her 'fence training' went well. She responded to our warning calls each time she got too close to it, realising that the fence was bad.

Sally had also gone through an amazing transformation. The first time I had met her she was a stubborn and naughty infant who abused her human caretakers with her disobedience. Now she had quietened down, paid attention to communications from her caretakers and constantly needed their reassurance, which is just what the nature of a young chimp should be like.

Next it was Zeena's turn. As I've mentioned, she had shown no inclination to engage in acceptance behaviour and never wanted reassurance from her human caretakers, so we were not sure how this was going to work out. I positioned myself inside the enclosure and Phillip stationed himself in the space between the adult camp and the infant camp in case Zeena mistakenly made her way through the second fence and into the enclosure with Abu and the other big boys. Sally had now been returned to one of the introduction rooms, so Zeena was the only one in the large room of the sleeping quarters. As soon as we opened the hatch Zeena darted out as though she was being chased by a guard dog. She pulled up about ten yards into the enclosure. What little hair remained on her was standing erect, clearly showing the stress she was experiencing. I didn't try to pursue her, but everyone present began talking to her calmly.

'It's okay, Zeena,' I said, hoping she'd head for the forest rather than the fence. Instinctively, it seemed she decided to do the opposite and ran towards the fence. The enclosure had only been recently completed and our initial design did not include the wire mesh to be placed outside the electric fence below ground level which meant that there were small spaces of up to three inches at certain places where the ground was uneven. Zeena was the one to point out this weakness to us. She flattened herself and used her momentum to get under the lowest strand of electrified fencing. The twelve thousand volt shock at thirty joules was enough to knock a grown man off his feet and it gave Zeena a considerable jolt. She released an enormous scream but her momentum was enough to propel her through to the other side of the fence into the space between the two enclosures. It was anyone's guess what she would do next.

Unwilling to go to Phillip, she stopped halfway between the two enclosures. A mere 30 feet separated the fences of the two enclosures. I left the enclosure as fast as I could through an access gate and made my way across to help Phillip. He was standing between Zeena and the adult enclosure to ensure that she didn't go that way. I could see that she wasn't at all happy; she was screaming, hair erect. It would be only a matter of time before she did something wrong. I decided to open a door to the sleeping quarters; it was the only part of the strange environment that she was familiar with. Then I walked towards her, holding out my hand and hunching over so that I was at her level. We needed to calm her down and get her to follow me but she remained reluctant to allow any contact with me. Changing tactics, I walked up to her, calling her to follow me, and then turned and walked rapidly towards the sleeping quarters. She hesitated for a second and then seemed to realise that this was the only way back to her group. I walked into the room and she followed a few feet behind. Once inside she jumped on to the mesh windows that separated the main room from the introduction room. It was an attempt to be reunited with her comrades, the ones she had previously shown no interest in.

Zeena was a strange chimp and difficult to understand. In the end I came to the conclusion that she desperately wanted to be part of a group but had serious trust issues with both humans and chimps. Many years later, and after many more chimps had joined the group, her behaviour finally changed for the better. One thing was certain: her traumatic early life and negative interactions with humans made her rehabilitation a lengthy process. But we managed to provide her with the right circumstances: three key things – space, friendship and behavioural enrichment – changed her into a chimpanzee who would become a significant member of her group.

Last one up was Cozy. For me this was a moment that embodied everything we stood for. Seven chimpanzees had arrived at Chimp Eden since our rescue efforts began and they were all equally deserving of what we could offer them. But Cozy was different for me. Perhaps it was because he was the first chimp I bonded with; perhaps it was because he responded to me differently from the way he responded to anyone else; or perhaps it was because I was with him all the way on his journey to freedom.

Sally and Zeena were separated in the introduction rooms and I entered the main room which now had only Cozy in it. He was in a playful mood and I spent about fifteen minutes with him before the hatch was opened. There are a few experiences I look back on that define my life, that give it meaning and substance. This was one of them and I will cherish the memory of it for the rest of my life. I went back out through the hatch and moved to one side to allow Cozy to leave the room. He stuck his head out of the doorway and gazed in bewilderment at the natural beauty around him. Only Cozy will know what was going through his mind at that moment but the expression of amazement on his face said it all for me.

'*Argghh,*' he said, his signature expression.

I stood upright and led him into the enclosure. He put his hand in mine and we walked towards the forest. He moved slowly, like an old man. Up to that point, none of us had thought about the effect of the harsh sun and uneven terrain on his pale skin and soft feet and this was clearly uncomfortable for Cozy. The enclosure has a variety of flora. The southern side has eucalyptus and jacaranda trees with Kikuyu grass growing in patches. To the west is an open field with indigenous spear grass. The eastern and northern sides have indigenous trees and a large lawn of Kikuyu in front of the tourist day visit centre. The southern side also linked the enclosure with the sleeping quarters and this was Cozy's first contact with the African soil. A huge jacaranda tree, about fifty feet high, is the closest tree to the sleeping quarters and when we reached it Cozy dropped my hand and investigated it. He leaned against the tree and looked up the length of the trunk into the maze of branches. I imagined he was wondering what it would be like to swing among those beautiful branches, something he wasn't capable of at that stage. I asked him to follow me and he backed away from the tree and took my hand once more. We walked around the enclosure for about an hour before returning to the sleeping quarters.

The day might have come to an end for Sally, Zeena and Cozy, but their journey was just beginning.

The next day we opened the hatch and released all three chimps from their sleeping quarters. Zeena had learned her lesson and didn't try to escape again. She headed straight for the trees and straight up the jacaranda, which would prove to be a favourite with every chimp that joined this group. Phillip joined us in the enclosure and Cozy relished the extra attention. Sally became more confident and spent most of her time up the jacaranda and adjacent eucalyptus. Cozy returned to the jacaranda and once again gazed up the trunk into the branches. He had had a lot of practice climbing in quarantine, but this was different and a lot more difficult for him.

I decided to make this part of his daily routine and climbed into the tree. About four feet up I stopped and positioned myself in such a way that I could reach down and offer him a hand. He was only too glad to take my hand when he realised that I was going to pull him up into the tree. He weighed between 55 and 75 pounds so it wasn't difficult to pull him up to my level. He looked nervous but none the less pleased with himself. He was also very cautious, either holding on to me or the branch below him. He didn't try to clamber about, but he was at peace studying his environment and shouting warnings at Sally and Zeena every time they came too close.

During the next few months I would climb with Cozy on an almost daily basis and he always preferred that particular jacaranda. The climbing technique he developed was a bit odd because he tried to copy the only climbing style I could show him. With only two hands and no opposable thumbs on my feet, I could only teach him to climb the same way I did. Over time he would learn to use his feet to his advantage and after about two years he was climbing some of the highest trees in the enclosure. He finally became a real chimpanzee.

In time, many more chimpanzees joined the group, until eventually there were thirteen in all. Two adult chimps also joined the group, Joao and Zac. It turned out that Joao was not happy living under Abu's rule and he tried to escape numerous times. We decided to introduce him to the infant group and following the 'mediation' technique in time he accepted the others, eventually becoming the uncontested alpha male.

For almost two years I spent as much time as I could with the group teaching them skills through repetitive actions. When Zac was introduced my role changed. Joao, now a fearless leader demanding respect from everyone, including me, objected to my frequent presence in the enclosure because of the complex social hierarchy situation with the newcomer Zac. When Joao made his intentions clear it was a bittersweet moment for me. On the one hand, I was sad to leave the group, knowing that I would never again be able to spend one-on-one time with Cozy. On the other hand, I was proud to know that I'd played an important part in establishing a group which initially had been unable to do without human help and now didn't require it at all. I would go on to rescue many more chimpanzees but Cozy remains my greatest achievement and my best friend.

NINE
ANGOLA OR BUST

Going back to the time before Cozy's rescue, there was one mission in particular that stood out for me. My visit to Angola in 2005 had confirmed my personal commitment to rescue every last captive chimpanzee in Luanda, no matter how long it took.

I had learned of the change of heart of the Angolan director of forestry when I returned home with Cozy. Two of the original nine chimps in Luanda had died unexpectedly only days apart – Bebe and Virgilio. Negotiations with GAP Brazil were taking a long time to finalise and the director had become anxious that more chimps would die. He had therefore decided to contact us again.

This meant that immediately after my return from Italy I had to travel to Angola to bring back Sally during which time Phillip took delivery of Zeena, the infant chimpanzee from the United Arab Emirates.

Sally's previous caretaker, Josephine Pickles, introduced me to some valuable contacts when I was relocating Sally. Her help was undoubtedly instrumental in ensuring my success in getting Sally flown out at the first attempt, and I was most grateful to her for her connections and persistence in obtaining the relevant documents from the relevant state departments.

After seeing Sally safely relocated to Chimp Eden I went to Mozambique to arrange the relocation of Joao. Once these missions had been completed I returned to Angola to tackle the urgent matter of the remaining Angolan chimps. They couldn't be moved at the same time as Sally because the construction of their crates had not been completed in time.

With these missions lined up, I had spent hardly any time at home. The relocation of all the captive Angolan chimpanzees to Chimp Eden was now being described as 'urgent' by the director of forestry and I was under pressure to get the job done as quickly as possible.

One chimp was of particular concern. My friend Lucinda Piets had informed me that on a visit to Maquil, the hardware store holding the chimp named Lika, she had discovered that a large generator was venting its exhaust fumes directly into Lika's cage and that this had caused her to lose condition very rapidly. My obvious response was to demand that the generator be moved until I could organise the relocation of Lika and Lucinda confirmed later that this had been done. However, we could not assess what damage Lika might already have suffered and it was imperative to get her out of Angola as quickly as possible.

In anticipation of the rescue mission and relocations we had built five travel crates and shipped them to Angola. We didn't expect there to be any problems with this as the crates were empty apart from containing a single blanket each.

The first challenge Murphy's Law threw at me was that I couldn't find a veterinarian to assist me with the relocation. Dr Stephen van der Spuy would only be able to assist in the taking of blood samples. The best alternative I could find was a South African medical doctor resident in Angola and I enlisted his help. Although there were strict regulations that specified that only a South African veterinarian could be involved in the operation, I managed to obtain special permission to use the services of a medical doctor. The reason for the regulations was that the Department of Agriculture Veterinary Services need to be sure that legally they are in a position of authority over the contracted veterinarian. The falsification of blood samples and veterinary assistance in the smuggling of animals is not unknown. Dr Mouton freelanced for a medical evacuation company in Luanda and he was happy to assist, provided he didn't have to do the actual darting. Because the physiology of a chimpanzee was similar to that of a human being the same drugs could be used on both species, although they were sold under different names. Dr Mouton could therefore supply the drugs and I would take care of the darting.

When I left for Angola at the end of July 2006, the plan was as follows. Dr van der Spuy would fly to Angola and, with the help of Lucinda Piets, immobilise all the chimps that were to be relocated and take blood samples. Our clearing agent in Luanda would clear the crates at the airport and transport them to a safe house which was being provided by Sally's former caretakers. I would focus on only five of the six chimpanzees as the owner of the sixth chimp didn't want to part with his animal and had applied for a permit to keep Josephine.

The blood sample results should take no longer than six days before they were available from the Biomedical Primate Research Centre in Amsterdam. Having visited all the chimp locations and being aware of the logistical constraints in moving around Luanda, I had planned everything to the very last detail, including the time schedule, the actual route we would take through the city, and the details regarding the check-in of the animals at the airline cargo facility.

I had identified a few problem areas as far as my plan was concerned, and the Customs and airline cargo check-in were at the top of the list. In an attempt to combat corruption in the import and export processes, the Angolans had instituted a system whereby shipping agents had to submit detailed paperwork on the shipment forty-eight hours in advance, but after that there was no further communication between the Customs officials and the shipping agent during the forty-eight-hour period. What this meant was that if there were any problems with the paperwork I wouldn't have a second chance. The mission would have to be scrapped and I would have to start all over again, beginning with new blood samples. This would mean that the departure date would be delayed for two weeks, not to mention the enormous costs involved in having to bring a veterinarian back to Angola to take the blood samples.

Once Customs has approved the paperwork there was a general to and fro-ing between Customs, the national airline TAAG and the shipping agent's office, all of which were located within a radius of 800 yards of one another. (This part of the process isn't recommended for the unfit and a strong stomach is also required as Luanda doesn't have many sewerage systems in working order. Luandans seem to have adapted well – so well, in fact, that in general people did their 'business' in the street simply adding to inches of foul sewage already accumulated there.)

What with payments, receipts, copies, and crate weighing completed in a day, and with only seconds to spare before take-off, the mission had the mental and physical effects of a day in a military boot camp. When I was relocating Sally, I was able to persuade the airline to allow us to take her to the airport at 3am to be loaded on to the aircraft that would depart around 8am. Check-in was no walk in the park either. Challenges ranged from dealing with security to Customs officers looking for bribes to the incompetence of the cargo-loading personnel who always seemed to have problems with the paperwork.

On my second mission I wouldn't be so lucky as to organise check-in in the early hours of the morning because of the distances between the three rescue locations. A distance of ten miles could easily take four hours in the congested traffic of Luanda which only seemed to quieten down between midnight and 2am.

It was the end of July when I made my way to Luanda on the rescue mission. I had been there several times during the last year, but this time would be different. I was excited about bringing out all the chimps I had committed myself to saving on my first visit. I was also very tired after almost two months of work that had been both difficult and draining, to say the least. We had had some remarkable successes, most notably Cozy. But this mission, with five chimps involved, promised to be the mother of all rescues. But I am not one to shy away from a challenge, so I breathed deeply and told myself, 'What will be, will be.'

After the four-hour flight I landed in Luanda late in the evening. Grinaker-LTA, the company that had given me a place to operate from, had sent a driver to pick me up. The eight-mile drive between the airport and the Grinaker staff compound took about an hour. When I was delivered to my three-bedroom wooden house I noticed that something was missing. The crates were not there. They were supposed to have been cleared by the agent the same day I arrived and delivered to the house.

I immediately phoned our shipping agent Tom. Born and raised in

Angola, Tom had learned to survive by wheeling and dealing on the streets and he had accumulated contacts everywhere imaginable. An extremely nice person, he was also a cunning salesman who could probably sell sand to an Arab.

'Tom,' I said, 'the crates aren't here at the house. Where are they?'

'We get them tomorrow,' he replied. 'I meet you at the airport and we get them then, okay?'

'That wasn't the arrangement, Tom. What happened?'

'Customs people are being difficult, but you can explain to them about the monkey rescue.'

'Are you saying they might not release the crates?' I was getting anxious.

'No, no, NO! It will be fine.'

'Okay, then. I'll see you tomorrow.'

There was no point in arguing with Tom over the phone but my heart sank at his news because without the crates there was no way I would be moving the chimps. I couldn't understand why there should be a problem because I had negotiated the process perfectly well when I sent Sally's crate ahead of me. No alarm bells were rung on that occasion.

The next morning I left the Grinaker complex early, anticipating a two-hour drive ahead of me. I could probably have covered the eight miles faster on foot. The slow-moving traffic resulted in a dense layer of carbon dioxide hanging over the city which instantly gave me a splitting headache and an uncomfortable feeling of nausea. As we parked the car in front of the cargo department I phoned Tom who told me to meet him at the entrance to the Customs department. On the previous trip I had learned that Customs officials never allow just anyone to enter their lair, much less talk to them face-to-face.

Tom was on time. Although I was concerned about the non-clearance of the crates, it was still good to see him. Our earlier adventures with Sally had obviously had a bonding effect and if this new mission was to have any chance of succeeding we would have to be on the same team all the way.

Tom pressed a buzzer at the gate that led to an entrance at the back of the building. A security guard in khaki glared at us suspiciously but finally an overweight lady in the blue uniform of a Customs official arrived and Tom started his magic. In no time at all we were ushered into the office where paperwork was handled and invited to sit down on two small chairs that had seen better days. Tom's 'contact' then arrived, a tall woman who had an air of authority about her. She was extremely friendly towards Tom and I had to wonder how he had gone about making her one of his contacts. He was jabbering away in Portuguese like a jet engine in full thrust; she was listening and looking at the papers he had presented her with.

Tom might have been a smooth operator, but officialdom remained officialdom. His contact lifted her hand to stop him talking. She asked a few questions which Tom seemed too embarrassed to answer. She didn't look convinced by anything he said. Then she sighed, got up from her chair and left the room.

'Are you going to tell me what the hell this is all about?' I asked.

'She says her superiors do not understand why empty boxes were imported. It doesn't make sense to them and it smells like a ... how you say? ... a scam.'

'What are you talking about? Show her the CITES permits I sent you, it's an animal rescue that has been endorsed by an Angolan ministry.'

'I showed her the permits, but her boss no believe.'

After about thirty minutes the woman returned but she didn't sit down. Tom stood up instead and she started her explanation with a serious expression on her face.

Eventually, Tom said, 'Okay, let's go.'

Once outside, he elaborated while referring to the piece of paper she had given him.

'She says they don't trust us and will keep the crates until they figure out what's going on. Either that or we pay five thousand dollars which is a value calculated on the airline shipping costs.'

'This is horseshit, brother! I will get the director of the department of forestry to sort them out. Now let's get out of here. I have to go see one of the chimps.'

I was furious because I hadn't seen it coming. Tom had insisted everything would be okay and I'd had no reason to doubt him. Without the crates the mission would have to be called off. After the series of missions we'd recently completed, JGI South Africa didn't have the budget to pay the five thousand dollars.

'This is Africa' was the thought that came to mind as I contemplated the sort of corruption one so frequently encounters in Africa. Another thought, 'Africa wins again', followed the first, both aptly describing the likely outcome of trying to carry out complicated operations in Africa. I don't like losing and there was no chance I was leaving without a fight. It was too early in the morning to confront anyone in the government buildings in downtown Luanda, but I would be able to do something else in the meanwhile: visit Lika. We set off for the Maquil hardware store where I had visited her a number of times before.

From the outside nothing much about the hardware store had changed. The big metal door was still in place shielding the interior. I knocked on the side door and a security guard opened it for me. Lika's cage was only fifteen yards from the door and the space in front of it, which had previously been empty, was now occupied by a large generator. One could never be certain of the power supply in Luanda, but it was working today and the generator was silent. I noticed that the generator's exhaust pipes were pointing away from Lika's cage. I walked up to the cage and she emerged from its dark interior. '*Argh argh argh*,' I said softly and she returned my greeting.

I didn't sense any danger so I went close to the bars and gave her the opportunity to groom my arm, which she did. Lika was a pretty chimp, but very emaciated. There was no telling what harm she had suffered from the exhaust fumes constantly pouring into her cage. All we could do was get her to Chimp Eden as soon as possible and put her into the hands of the experts to nurse her back to top condition.

Lika's owner, Mr da Silva, was at the store and he joined me at Lika's cage. He still seemed as sympathetic as he had been on my first visit to Luanda some time ago and he described his problems to me. Because of the small size of the shop there was nowhere else to place the generator but he had realised the mistake he had made with the venting of the fumes into Lika's cage. He had immediately made a plan to divert the exhaust pipes. Mr da Silva was an old man and I had learned a while ago that he was not in good health. He had been one of the most avid supporters of Lika's move to Chimp Eden.

During the Angolan civil war and the country's subsequent isolation from the rest of the world, people bought chimpanzees and other endangered species from the markets in an effort to save their lives, or because they realised they were probably doomed if they were sold for reasons other than the pet trade. People like Mr da Silva believed that he was saving Lika from a worse fate, yet in the end he wasn't able to offer her a better life and she ended up in the most appalling conditions. I have no doubt that he was ignorant of the fact that he was condemning her to a life of misery in that small cage and that, as a wild animal, she had highly specialised needs. At least, though, his motives were sincere and he did not try to profit from her as so many others did.

Mr da Silva could not speak a word of English and used a translator to tell me that I really needed to get Lika out as soon as possible because he could no longer take care of her. It seemed to me that if Lika stayed neither of them might see the end of the year. I desperately wanted her out of the cage and on a flight to Chimp Eden but unless I could organise for the crates to be released from Customs there was not much chance I would be able to do anything for her.

'Please tell Mr da Silva that I will get her out in the next week,' I said to the translator. I felt compelled to commit to this, although in reality there were no guarantees, thanks to the ignorance of the Customs department.

I left the Maquil hardware store with renewed determination to retrieve the crates and went directly to the department of forestry. I managed to get a meeting with Dr Almeida who was furious, to say the least, when he heard what had happened. I agreed to take responsibility for organising a letter from the director of the department and, feeling confident that I was going about this the right way, I moved on to the next step.

The mission schedule was tight and there really was no room for error.

Stephen had taken the blood samples fifteen days earlier and that left me with just four days before another problem would catch up with me: the twenty-one-day blood sample validity period. There was no way around this; no matter how much I grovelled the state vet wasn't going to budge on this one.

I spent most of the next day in and out of the Customs building, until we were finally kicked out after I brought in Dr Almeida to apply pressure. I had now exhausted this option and it was made plain to me that they weren't going to budge even if the president himself showed up to plead my case. The crates would stay where they were until they figured out what my 'scam' was.

The fact that the chimpanzees had to be moved to South Africa as a matter of urgency, and that I had all the permits required, made absolutely no impression on their attitude. They would not change their decision to keep the crates – unless, of course, we came up with the five thousand dollars. I felt completely shattered when I walked out of the Customs office. I walked slowly to the kerb where I sat down, a feeling of helpless nausea engulfing me. I had promised Mr da Silva that Lika would leave and, by implication, that she would survive and be cared for at Chimp Eden. I was no longer sure that would happen. I rested my head on my knees, trying to think what to do next. Customs was not going to give me my crates and without the crates I had no other way of moving the chimps ... or did I?

I had heard of people who experience moments of great clarity when under extreme stress, although I couldn't recollect ever having had that feeling myself. Well, not until that moment. It hit me like a silver bullet.

'Tom,' I said, 'screw those crates! I'm going to build new ones!'

'There's no time,' he said. 'We have to hand in the paperwork tomorrow or you won't get to leave on time.'

'That's where you are wrong, my friend. All we need to do is persuade the airline to take the weight of our confiscated crates and then you will have all you need to draw up the export documentation. Leave the crate building to me.'

Tom stared at me and then burst out laughing. 'You are crazy, mzungu! Why are you doing this? They're only monkeys!'

'Wrong again. And you *are* going to help me.'

Cunning he might have been, but Tom was a pretty nice guy and I knew that he would follow through. He just needed a gentle push.

'Okay, we do it,' he said, shaking his head. 'You are still crazy.'

'Cool, brother. You go ahead and sweet talk the ladies at the airline and I'll do my thing.'

Tom walked off with a grin on his face, probably thinking that none of this was going to materialise. Angola operated very much on 'island time' and it took weeks to get anything done. Building five crates in three days didn't seem feasible.

I began pacing up and down the parking lot, thinking about where to start. I had no equipment, no materials and no help. Then it dawned on me that the one person I was trying to help also had the means to help me build the crates. Mr da Silva. I had noticed that the Maquil hardware store was wall-to-wall with equipment, especially items that could make the job go a lot faster. I asked the driver to get us there as quickly as possible.

Although Maquil had the equipment I still lacked the raw materials

– pressed wood, steel rods, wire mesh, to name but a few. When you worked in a place like Angola you came to appreciate the convenience of having a hardware store on every corner at home. Every time I returned to South Africa I got the overwhelming urge to get down on my knees and kiss the ground as soon as I stepped off the plane. There was no other country in Africa like it. Angola might have a way to go before it catches up, but it wasn't wasting time getting there. There were construction sites all over the place which was one of the main reasons the traffic was so congested. That, and the fact that there wasn't a single traffic light in a city with a population of more than two million.

On our way to Maquil we had to negotiate extensive roadworks. A Caterpillar grading machine wasn't helping by being stationary in one of the two traffic lanes. Not surprisingly, there was no traffic officer to assist motorists. When our turn arrived to overtake the grader I noticed a Barlow World sticker on its side.

'That's it!' I yelled, startling the driver out of his wits. 'That's how we are going to get the chimps out!'

The driver looked at me as if I was a man possessed.

'Turn the car round and go to the Barlow World outlet ... you know where it is?'

The driver nodded and turned off into a side street to avoid having to backtrack through the traffic we had just negotiated. My idea was simple, daring, maybe dangerous and I wasn't sure whether or not it was workable: I wanted to use diesel engine shipping crates and convert them into travel crates for the chimps. Crates built to transport almost a ton of metal would surely be strong enough to hold a chimp, even though certain adjustments would have to be made. There was only one way to find out and we'd have a headstart instead of having to start from scratch.

I arrived at the Barlow World outlet and service centre just before closing time. While waiting at the front reception desk I was recognised by a man who walked up and greeted me. It was my old friend Billa who knew my reason for being in Angola only too well – he had taken care of Sally when Phillip and I were forced to leave the country. Perhaps Murphy was giving me a break for the first time on this mission? It seemed that Billa had left Grinaker shortly after his spell of chimp-minding and had joined Barlow World where he was working in logistics. He agreed to help me with locating empty crates. When I told him why I needed them, he gave me a wide-eyed look and chuckled.

Construction was definitely the right business to be in in Angola – we walked through the servicing facility past so many newly imported machines that I lost count. When we arrived at the back of the facility Billa pointed out three large crates. After inspecting them thoroughly my spirits lifted as I visualised what they would look like when I'd finished working on them.

The crates were made of pinewood, but the panels were thick and strong. Their dimensions were slightly larger than our crates, which made them ideal. Barlow didn't need the crates and I could have them immediately and free of charge. I phoned Mr da Silva and explained briefly what I was trying to do and asked if I could take him up on his offer of help. Without delay he dispatched his truck to transport the crates back to Maquil. Barlow World was closing just then, so I moved all the crates to the sidewalk while I waited for the truck. I settled myself on top of one of them, took out my notebook and began to draw up a list of everything I would need for modifying the crates so that they would be suitable for the chimps.

I also started thinking about the decisions I would soon have to make.

Three crates meant only three chimps would be going back. In simple terms, this meant choosing the most desperate cases, the ones who would likely not survive until I could return, which might be as long as three months. Virgilio, one of the chimps at the liqueur bottling factory had died; originally there had been three but Virgilio had escaped and the panic-stricken workers had given the chimp an overdose of sleeping pills which resulted in her death. Was it conceivable that this could also happen to the remaining two chimps? These two, Mimi and Xinga, had been in their cage for more than eleven years. On the other hand Zac, the chimp at the nightclub, was extremely emaciated and didn't look as though he'd last much longer. He had been outside the nightclub for seventeen years, chained to a single tree for most of that time, and he had endured unbelievable suffering.

A second of the original nine Angolan chimps had died. This was the five-year-old female named Bebe who had been chained to a tree adjacent to Zac. She had been in good physical condition the last time I saw her and her unexpected death from severe diarrhoea and dehydration could only be attributed to negligence on the part of her owner.

Then there was Lika. Her living quarters and poor physical condition meant she was probably the most worrying case of all. But in reality all were equally deserving of leaving Angola on this mission. How was I going to choose? And how would I deal with the guilt if one of them died in Angola before I could return? The arrival of the truck meant I had to put these agonising thoughts on hold. I had to focus on doing what I could, and there was no time to waste.

The two men who arrived in the truck helped me to load the crates, each of which weighed in the region of 150 to 200 pounds. After the ninety-minute drive to Maquil and the offloading of the crates there was no time to organise the workers and the equipment I would need. I would have to be content with starting work on the crates the next day and the extent of the resources at Maquil would determine whether or not this was a hare-brained idea.

I was up at 4am the next day and started the arduous journey through Luanda's traffic. I was nervous and impatient – every minute on the road was one less to get the job done. There are few things in life that drive me bonkers, but one of them is the feeling of helplessness that comes with not being in control, or having to depend on circumstances that are beyond my control. I reflected that driving in slow-moving traffic was one of the reasons I didn't fit into life in the city: people rushing, exhaust fumes and noise were all elements I couldn't cope with for very long – it just wasn't programmed into my DNA. Most people would rather not be marooned on a desert island – I would relish the prospect.

The journey took just less than two hours and already the hot Angolan sun was beating down. But at last I had the chance of trying to get the mission back on track. During the next twenty-four hours I would have to complete work on the crates, get the paperwork from Tom and, hopefully, with the help of Dr Mouton I could start the road trip through Luanda to immobilise and load the three chimps that would be returning to Chimp Eden. At that point I had not yet made any decisions about who would go and who would stay.

Maquil had no shortage of equipment or materials and I was soon walking up and down the aisles gathering up what was needed. Self-tapping screws, steel rods, welding rods, hinges and a long list of power tools were but a few of the items I selected. The only space I could find to work in was at the entrance, close to Lika's cage.

The crates needed a lot of work. First, I had to sand them down to remove dangerous splinters. Then I needed to build a cage of steel rods and wire mesh that would fit inside the wooden crate and stand on top of a drainage pan that would collect the chimp's faeces and urine during transport. Mr da Silva was kind enough to provide me with a few skilled workers and we sprang into action. Lika seemed to enjoy watching us sweat in the sun – there was no roof covering in that part of the hardware store – and from time to time she'd comment with a hoot. It was as if she was urging us on.

We had to focus on modifying all three crates at the same time and by closing time at 5pm the steel cage frames were complete and the crates looked more like something that could be used to transport an animal rather than a diesel engine. Although there was still much to do the next day, I felt confident that the team would be able to finish the job by noon. I had not heard from Tom during the day and my attempts to contact him that evening were futile. If Tom didn't get an answer from Customs by 5pm the next day all my efforts would come to nothing.

I hardly slept that night. The number of factors that could still affect the relocation of the chimps was weighing heavily on me. So, rather than tossing and turning all night, I put the hours to use practising my darting skills with the blowpipe. I mounted a target on the inside of the front door and practised at close range. The blowpipe was surprisingly accurate over short distances; the question was, would it do it in reality?

A blowpipe wasn't the obvious first choice as a darting device. But it passed through airport security without comment whereas the Dan-Inject gun we usually used bore rather too close a resemblance to an assault rifle.

I was up at 4am the next day and departed once again for Maquil to complete the work on the crates. All the workers were ready and waiting for the final effort and I depended on them to get the work done. Around 10am I took a break from the work which was progressing well and phoned Tom. He answered this time, but he didn't have any good news for me just yet. He told me that he had handed in the paperwork, but it was usual for it only to be released in the afternoon. He would wait at his delivery box at the entrance to the Customs building to find out whether or not our application had been successful.

I had gone through this process with him before and knew how tedious and tense the waiting could be. It was a hot, humid room that looked something like a post office: two walls made up of hundreds of tiny doors which each opened into a box into which the accepted or rejected applications were placed. Every export company had a runner standing close to their box listening for the documents to be dropped into them. Even with all his 'contacts', Tom was subjected to the same tiresome wait.

By 4pm the crates were ready. For a job that had been completed in just two days I felt pretty proud and so did my helpers. Dr Mouton had made his way to Maquil and had already prepared Lika's immobilisation dart. He had never prepared a dart for a chimpanzee before but he seemed confident, checking and rechecking his equipment and dosage calculations.

Everything was in place. All the Maquil staff were standing around, some of them taking the time to say goodbye to Lika. She had spent almost her entire life in this small cage. Most of the workers had seen her every working day and many of them had interacted with her in some way or other. In essence, she was a fixture and with her gone the place would never be the same for them again.

In situations like this I always have very conflicting emotions. On the one hand, I was angry that Lika had been kept in such a small cage for such a long time suffering both physical and mental damage from which she might never recover. On the other hand, I had got to know some of the staff the last few days and there was a spirit of camaraderie arising from our shared efforts to create suitable travel crates out of pinewood boxes. As with Svetlana, Mr da Silva and his staff didn't strike me as evil people, they didn't profit materially from Lika's presence and weren't using her to entice more customers to visit the store. I guess each of us has to form our own opinion about whether these owners were bad or ignorant or misguided. All I know is that then and there I felt sorry that they had to say goodbye to an animal that had been part of their lives for so long. Mr da Silva, a frail old man, took his time saying an emotional farewell to Lika.

Just before 5pm I got the call from Tom.

'Hey, man, I have bad news for you.'

My heart sank. During the last two days I had convinced myself that we were going to succeed.

'Talk to me,' I said, turning away from the others.

'I got the paperwork out of Customs. It is approved. But the assholes have only just finished it and now it's late and the airline people have closed up and gone home.'

'This can't be happening. Are you telling me that TAAG is the reason we can't get the chimps out of here?'

'Yes.'

'I'll get the TAAG boss on the line. Don't leave the airport.'

I hurriedly dug in my bag looking for a business card that had been given to me some time ago at a dinner party in South Africa. It was that of the head of the TAAG cargo division in South Africa. Within minutes I had him on the phone and outlined the importance and urgency of my problem. He in turn phoned the head of TAAG airline in Luanda, who phoned me back – all in less than fifteen minutes. Only when he told me that nothing could be done did I accept the fact that Lika and the others wouldn't be leaving for Chimp Eden.

One of the most difficult aspects of working in countries like Angola is the lack of options. TAAG held sole rights for exporting cargo out of the country so even if I could find another airline willing to assist me at short notice, it would not be allowed to do so. We had missed our only flight option for at least another seven days and this would take us past the validity period for the blood tests.

It was the lowest of all low points for me; I couldn't remember ever having felt so helpless. If I failed now Lika might no longer be alive when I returned. But regardless of my emotional state I had to walk back to a room full of people and tell them that it had all been for nothing. The first person I told was Mr da Silva. I don't think that I will ever forget the expression on his face when he realised that Lika wasn't going to leave – it was one of utter disappointment and sadness.

I spent some time apologising but it didn't make up for shattering everyone's expectations. The best I could hope for now was that Lika would survive the three months before I could return. I made arrangements for the drugs, darts and crates to be stored safely and then left the hardware store. I sat down on the kerb outside, my head slumped between my knees. I was angry and tired, but I was unwilling to accept defeat. This time around it wasn't Lebanese gangsters or politicians that had got the better of me, but a country that was working against itself. I knew that I had done everything I possibly could, but that only made me feel worse. Would I be able to get it right the next time?

I returned home empty-handed and sick with disappointment, but with an anger that gave me renewed determination. I was angry mostly because I couldn't limit the factors that were outside my control – or that were susceptible to Murphy's Law which seemed to follow me everywhere. Most people interpret this Law as 'if anything can go wrong, it will' but in my case it was more like 'if anything can go wrong, it will do so *at the same time as everything else*'. I had reached a critical stage in my thinking. I would either have to give up or I would have to radically change the way I planned missions, particularly in regard to dealing with Murphy's Law. I needed to formulate my plans in such a way that for every Plan A there would be both a Plan B *and* a Plan C in place.

By the end of October, the quarantined chimps had been moved to their new enclosures and I left for Angola for another attempt. This time round I made different plans.

First, instead of sending crates to Luanda I would have additional crates made through another of Tom's contacts, thereby bypassing Customs altogether. It was reasonable to expect that Murphy's Law would come into play and that something would go wrong with the construction of the crates, so I decided to take with me all the materials needed to build a crate from scratch just to sidestep that possibility.

Next, blood samples had to be taken and sent to the laboratory in Amsterdam. This was one of the factors that was outside my control but I planned to keep additional samples with me in case they disappeared in transit. Then we would bring in a second veterinarian to assist me with immobilisation and relocation: Dr Andre Beytell would arrive in Luanda just two days before departure. To ensure there would be no problems with export and health permits I made sure that the Angolan officials understood the urgent nature of the mission and realised that there would be repercussions if they didn't cooperate on time.

Exporting the chimps through Customs and the airline were other areas that were out of my control. The only back-up plan I could come up with was that I take one of them out of the equation. The airline was of course the one most likely to cooperate and this was done through proper discussions with the top officials at TAAG before I left for Angola. They agreed to extend me every courtesy, including keeping staff on overtime until all the paperwork and processes had been completed.

The final back-up plan was designed to raise the stakes. I asked South African television's leading wildlife investigative programme to join me on the mission. Cameraman Jacques Goosen would be accompanying me on behalf of the *50/50* production team. Their involvement would no doubt embarrass me if I failed yet again, but it would also serve to expose the sorts of issues that ultimately result in endangered species losing their lives.

And so the three of us left for Angola on an unforgettable adventure. Most people are in the habit of pointing out themselves in pictures of great holiday experiences; we would be pointing at pictures and saying of them 'we survived that night'.

I had arranged for Tom and Lucinda to take me to have a look at the newly built crates soon after I arrived. I had not invited Murphy to join us, but he was waiting there none the less for as soon as I set eyes on the crates I realised that it was time for Plan B to kick in. The crates were made of pressed wood that was one-third of the specified thickness and were far too weak to accommodate chimpanzees.

According to the builder, he'd used the best that was available in Luanda and it would just have to do. I asked Andre to proceed with the blood sampling while I focused on getting the cages up to specification. The materials I had brought with me would be adequate to make changes, but I knew there were some risks involved. With no wire mesh lining the inside of the crate the risk was not so much the possibility of a chimp escaping because the steel cage inside the crate was immensely strong; the risk was that the chimp could smash the wooden panels on the outside of the steel cage. The simplest option was just to install wire mesh but, believe it or not, the hardest thing to find in Luanda at that time was wire mesh (not to mention Band-Aids). I had to consider whether to postpone the mission yet again. But since there was no risk of the chimp escaping the steel cage, even though the crate was defective, I decided to go ahead.

The rest of the mission continued according to plan: every time Murphy threw a curve ball at me, I had a swing to match. Three days before departure date the blood samples were in, the permits were ready and Tom applied to Customs for our export permit the usual forty-eight hours before departure. Tom had mended his relationship with his contact and she sent him regular updates on progress.

All was looking good until one day before departure. That was when Tom had a phone call from his contact who explained that there was a 'complication' – one that could delay our mission once again. Because of a simple mistake on the exporter's code they were holding back approval. It was a déjà vu moment for me: I felt as if I was back in a situation of which I already knew the outcome. But this time round Plan B was there; in the cumbersome bag I was dragging around with me was a computer, a scanner and a printer. I quickly amended the document, buying just enough time to get it to Tom's contact. Just before 5pm we were called into the Customs Office to discuss our application. It was an unusual privilege to be called for a meeting, but it turned out to be more of an opportunity to rant, the Customs director being the one doing the ranting. Tom looked intimidated but since the rant was being conducted in Portuguese of which I didn't understand a word, there was no point in my feeling the same way.

'He says that they cannot approve this as there is not enough time,' was all that Tom translated.

At this point I had had enough of everything and I completely lost my temper.

'What the fuck do you want me to do before I can help you to rescue some of your own animals?' I shouted, standing up and kicking my chair over backwards 'Do you want me to do your work for you?'

I didn't hang around for a reply because I feared I might become violent. I had done everything humanly possible, planned everything down to the last detail, yet I couldn't get officials to do their work.

The director jumped up and began yelling at me, but I wasn't about to give him that satisfaction. 'Sorry, chief,' I said, 'but I have had enough of your bullshit. Get out of my way!'

I charged out of the office and headed for the car. The prospect of another mission failure was starting to sink in, but this time round there wouldn't be a follow-up, this was the last opportunity of getting the chimps out and I had failed. I got into the car and didn't bother giving the driver instructions.

'Just go ... just drive,' I said.

Cameraman Jacques Goosen was sitting in the back. He had documented all my activities during the last ten days and was extremely excited about filming the actual relocation.

'They have declined our export permit again,' was all I could manage to say.

'What? Are you serious? I can't believe it!'

He didn't bother to pick up his camera and film my reaction; he himself was too shocked that all our efforts had been in vain. No matter what part you play in a rescue mission, you can't help getting caught up in it.

'What do we do now?' Jacques asked.

'I don't know. I'm out of answers. I don't know if JGI will have the patience to try again. I'm afraid our time is up on this one.'

'Bliksem!' he said, an untranslatable Afrikaans expression that said it all.

My talk with Tom would have to wait for another day; things said in anger are always better left unsaid. We drove out of the parking lot and into the main road which was jammed with the slow-moving rush hour traffic. As I stared blindly out of the window, I suddenly saw a man leaping over the parking lot palisades, waving his arms wildly. It was Tom!

I got out of the car and ran to meet him.

'What's going on?' I asked, wondering if the Customs director was going to set the police on me.

'We have approval! We need to get to TAAG before they close!'

'What the hell …? What changed his mind?' I asked as we both ran towards the buildings, vaulting the palisades again to the disgust of the security guard.

'Your tantrum changed the director's mind,' he said with a big grin on his face.

'You screwing with me?' I asked. 'I'll kick your ass if you are!'

'Not a chance, chef. We have to hurry!'

The TAAG personnel weren't too happy to have us arriving in their office at 5.30pm but they had been told by management to stay on duty, if it was the last thing they did. If we hadn't made that arrangement, we'd surely have been stuffed.

While we waited for the paperwork to be processed I phoned the truck driver to pick me up as soon as we had all the documents in our hands. I also phoned Lucinda and asked her to inform all the owners to get ready for our arrival. The circular route we would take would begin with Club Hippico to pick up Zac and Guida, next would be Lika at Maquil, and last would be the liqueur bottling factory for Mimi and Xinga. Originally I had hoped to start with the chimp collection around midday but we now had only eight hours to get to the three different locations, immobilise five chimpanzees, get them settled in their travel crates and then get back to the airport before 3am.

With the documents in hand I left for the Grinaker compound on the back of the truck and we began the slow journey through Luanda's traffic. I felt that I was back in control. Although I was tense about all we still had to accomplish, I knew it was now up to us alone to determine whether or not we would succeed. I phoned Andre to tell him the good news but I could hear hesitation in his voice: he was worried about carrying out the immobilisation at night.

I was confident that we would manage and tried to reassure him by outlining the advantages. There would be less traffic than during the day, which would enable us to get to the chimp locations a lot more quickly, and it would be easier to approach the chimps because they would be blinded by the flashlight. I had done this many times in the past with my father, although admittedly with antelope and not intelligent primates.

When I arrived at Grinaker I found Lucinda and Andre ready and waiting. Andre was tense and uneasy. He took me aside.

'Eugene, are you sure you want to do this?' he said. 'I'm still nervous about darting at night.'

'We don't have a choice,' I told him firmly. 'This is the only way we are going to be able to get the chimps out of Angola. But you make the call when we get there, all right?'

In fact, it wasn't really my call at all and if there was any danger for the animals I wasn't going to push him. This seemed to reassure Andre to some degree.

The four of us and the two drivers loaded the crates on to the truck. Jacques got on to the back of the truck with me. Andre and Lucinda would follow us in the pickup truck. The traffic had cleared somewhat, enabling us to make good time to the first location, which we reached just before 8pm.

The owner, Mr Neves, was informed that we had arrived but didn't bother to come out to see the chimps off. To me, he was a typical tyrannical owner who kept the animals only because he hoped to make a profit out of them. Over the years he had had many chimpanzees chained to trees and, I had been told, the occasional gorilla was also on show from time to time. Most of them died from negligence in the terrible conditions in which they were kept. Zac was exceptional. He had survived malaria three times, despite the fact that he'd received very little treatment for it. The government had forced Mr Neves to give up the chimps after one of them had died because of the totally unacceptable way in which he was keeping them.

We stopped about twenty yards away from the chimps. They realised something was up and started vocalising and acting excitedly. They knew Lucinda well, and Guida in particular was very happy to see her.

'Make the call, Andre,' I said as the four of us gathered at the back of the pickup truck.

Looking at Guida, he said, 'I think we are good to go.'

In the meantime, Jacques had prepared his camera for night filming and it was already rolling. We decided to start with Guida. She was the less suspicious of the two chimps and she was relaxed with Lucinda around so we were able to use a less stressful strategy. Andre prepared a syringe and he and I discussed how we would go about things. We decided that Lucinda should reassure Guida while I manoeuvred myself behind her. I would then jab the syringe into her shoulder and inject all its contents. It took some persuasion on Lucinda's part to get Guida to calm down to the point where we could approach the two of them with upsetting her. As I jabbed the needle in her shoulder, she realised what was going on and, leaping off Lucinda's lap, she tried to chase Andre and me away.

After about five minutes the drug started to take effect and she rested her head on an old tractor tyre next to the tree. She was a beautiful young chimp who had so much to look forward to at Chimp Eden – just as long as nothing went wrong during the next few hours. I had known that Mr Neves would be uncooperative and so I fetched the bolt cutters from my bag. I cut the lock and removed the chain from around her neck. Friction from the chain had rubbed away all the hair on her neck, but these scars would disappear in time. I tried to imagine what it must have been like for her growing up with a heavy chain around her neck, but it was quite beyond me. Now, with the chain gone, how would she react? Would she freak out or would she be overjoyed?

Andre and I picked Guida up and placed her in the first crate on the back of the truck. We locked the crate door and Lucinda stayed with her to monitor her breathing by flashlight. Andre and I then moved on to Zac. He was known to be difficult and had bitten several people, including his owner, during the seventeen years he had been chained to his tree. I could make out his familiar shape under his blanket. He may have been in bad shape, but he wasn't prepared to be bullied by a bunch of strangers. In a single movement he tossed the blanket aside and charged at us, grabbing a handful of sand and throwing it at Jacques.

It was a direct hit on his fifty-thousand-dollar Sony camera. When he realised the camera had stopped functioning, Jacques let loose a string of expletives. He had not brought a spare camera, wanting to travel light and also avoid undue attention from the police who were always quick to extort money by threatening prison for breaking the law by filming 'sensitive government areas'. Fortunately, I had a small Sony PD150 video camera that Jacques could use as a substitute. It was clear that Zac wasn't going to make things easy for us. We were going to have to be very inventive if we were to dart him safely.

On my previous trip to Angola I had seen the limitations of the blow pipe. Although accurate, it wasn't ideal as the shooter needed to get as close as possible to the animal which put him at considerable risk. There were also risks to the animal if the dart were to strike the wrong part of the body, possibly penetrating a vital organ. Accuracy and distance were therefore of great importance.

Fortunately, Phillip had been able to devise a new type of collapsible rifle that received its charge from a foot pump rather than a carbon dioxide cylinder. The advantage of the new gun was that it resembled an air-pressurised paint spray gun rather than an assault rifle and thus aroused less interest from airport security. Andre would now have to point the rifle at Zac without the chimp realising what he was doing.

'I've got an idea that I think might give you an easier shot,' I told Andre.

'Let's hear it.'

'Take your headlamp off and shine it into Zac's eyes using one hand, and hold and fire the dart with the other hand. That way he won't see the gun and won't be jumping around trying to dodge the dart.'

'Okay, sounds like a good idea. Let's give it a bash.'

On that note, our plan was put into action. I approached Zac from the left shining my headlamp directly into his eyes, and Andre approached from the right. It was over in seconds without Zac suspecting anything. He only realised what had happened once the dart was protruding from his thigh.

Cutting the lock on Zac's neck was a great event for me. It had secured a chain for the better part of seventeen years and, from the look of it, I didn't think a key would have helped much in trying to open it. I think I did a good job hiding my emotions from the others but there was no denying that this was a huge moment for me. Here was a chimp who symbolised every evil that human beings had committed against the great apes. He was born and captured in the wild forests of Cabinda province, his family members most likely having been killed and sold as bush meat. Forced to survive on the generosity of partygoers at the club, he was given alcohol and cigarettes at times to entertain visitors. How he had managed to survive for so long when so many others had died in the same conditions was nothing short of miraculous. There was no doubt that Zac was a fighter and a survivor and the sky would be the limit as to what he could achieve and enjoy at Chimp Eden. Part of the promise to myself to bring out every last one of the captive Angolan chimps was fulfilled the moment the bolt cutters clamped down on the old metal lock. I would have liked to take time to savour the moment but we had a long way to go to collect the other chimps so we hurriedly loaded Zac into his crate along with a new blanket. There was no time to wait for him to wake up, so we would have to try to keep an eye on him as we drove to the next location.

It was just after 9.30pm when we set off for Maquil. The road would take us from Benfica to downtown Luanda and I was surprised to see that the streets were buzzing with life. The sidewalks lining the narrow roads were filled with barbecues and the smell of grilled chicken was thick in the air. After driving about a mile down a winding road the people on the sidewalks suddenly became hostile towards us and began throwing rocks at the truck, one missing my face by only a few inches.

The driver stuck his head out of the window and yelled, 'Get down, *now!*'

As one, Jacques and I fell down flat on the back of the truck. The reason for the aggression was not clear and it was worrying, to say the least. Most likely the partying people took exception to a pair of white guys standing on the back of a truck forcing its way through the narrow streets and disrupting their activities. But the truck soon began to speed up and I peered over the rail to find that we were now on a double-lane road that was free of both traffic and people.

An hour later we arrived at Maquil. This part of the city was mostly quiet with only a few people walking about. We pulled up at the entrance and Lucinda agreed to stay with her favourite chimps. Andre and I had both checked the chimps on the truck and both were awake but drowsy.

It was important to keep an eye on their breathing and to watch for any negative reaction to the drugs that might result in the animals vomiting. If the chimp's body was facing downward, there was a chance that vomit could enter the lungs which could result in death by asphyxiation.

We got our kit ready and went into the store to begin with Lika's immobilisation. It was something I had been looking forward to. Like Zac, Lika had survived her grim surroundings and the next step in her life could not have come a moment too soon. Only a few people were at the store – the security guard, Lika's caretaker and two other employees of Mr da Silva. The noise associated with the immobilisation of any animal is bound to attract the attention of people nearby, so it was a great advantage to have a quiet setting.

We first tried to inject Lika with a syringe but this failed because she became wise to our plan. Now suspicious of everyone, she was ready to grab anyone or anything that came too close. Darting was the only option so Andre prepared the dart. Lika's caretaker, a tall Angolan who had looked after her for most of her life, was one of the few people in the store who spoke English. This time we didn't have the advantage of darting from a distance under the light of the headlamps as the bars of the cage made it too dangerous to attempt.

Lika's cage was small and her movements would be restricted – at least that's what we thought at the outset. After more than thirteen years in the cage she sure knew how to make it almost impossible for Andre to get a clear shot for long enough. Because of the risk of a ricochet Andre had to get the muzzle past the steel bars, practically inside the cage, before taking the shot. Each time he did this Lika lunged forward, trying to grab the muzzle with the intention of pulling it into the cage. This frustrating behaviour continued for about ten minutes and each time she lunged towards the muzzle she screamed nervously. Her caretaker was becoming increasingly worried that Lika would manage to get hold of either the gun or Andre so he kept edging closer to the cage. At some point Lika made a very convincing attempt to grab the muzzle and the caretaker's instinctive action was to snatch the muzzle and pull it towards himself and away from Lika. A shot went off accidentally. Everyone froze and then looked around for the dart. To my utter horror I saw the dart sticking out of the caretaker's leg. Andre saw it at the same time and went white as a sheet. The only one who didn't seem too fazed was the caretaker himself.

'We have to get him off his feet,' Andre said.

'Sure. What's going to happen to him?'

'He should be okay once I give him the Antisedan for the Dormitol part of the cocktail,' Andre said, his voice urgent. He then took me aside and continued, 'There is nothing I can do about the ketamine. He's going to go on a wild trip.'

'Shit! Bugger!' I muttered helplessly. 'Anything else we can do?'

'Keep pouring water into his eyes once he's out,' Andre told me. 'They are going to dry out.'

'Has this ever happened before?' I asked.

'Yes, but not with me,' he said focusing his attention on the caretaker who was already showing signs of drowsiness.

I led the caretaker to the back of the hardware store and sat him down on the ground. Andre gave him the Antisedan that had been premixed for Lika. We stayed with him until he passed out. All the while Jacques had been busy filming, even capturing the actual moment the dart hit the caretaker's leg. Now I asked him to give the filming a rest and to take care of the guy who was drifting into unconsciousness.

'If there's no serious danger,' I said, 'why don't you prep another dart so that we don't lose too much time?'

'I agree,' Andre said and made his way to his kit at the entrance.

The biggest mistake we made throughout this whole ordeal was not to explain exactly what we were doing to the few Maquil workers who had been standing around, especially the security guard who seemed very upset about his comrade who had been 'shot'. At first we didn't notice too much going on, but that was because it had moved into the street. Andre, who was doing his prepping close to the door, was the first to hear the excited voices out on the kerb.

He walked over to me and said quietly, 'I think we have a problem.

Maybe you should check on what is going on outside.'

Andre asked the translator to put one of the workers in charge of monitoring the caretaker's breathing and we walked to the entrance. I peeked through an opening in the door at the small crowd of about ten people. They looked like ragtag individuals, some in military uniform and others looking pretty intoxicated. It struck me as the sort of mix that could be the perfect recipe for disaster. I went to our translator and asked him if he would call the security guard back into the building so that we could have a chat to him. As one of the intruders who had 'shot' his comrade I might not survive a hostile crowd.

I went back to Andre. 'We're going to have to speed things up,' I said. 'We may have outstayed our welcome.'

'Okay, I'm ready ... you ready?'

'Just give me a chance to talk to the security guard. Perhaps I can buy us some time before they string us up.'

After a short, heated discussion outside the translator and security guard walked through the entrance.

'He says you shot his friend,' the translator told me, looking very much as though he was taking the side of the security guard.

'Listen,' I said, 'and please translate this correctly. Your friend is fine, he just has some nice drugs in his system and is having a great time. He is going to wake up shortly.' I rolled my eyes in an attempt to illustrate someone high on drugs.

There was a short translation and then a further discussion between them.

'He is going to wake up soon?' the translator asked.

'Yes, yes, don't worry.'

The two of them looked as though they were convinced and they both left the building.

'Okay, let's get busy,' I said, running back to Andre.

I grabbed a blanket from the kit and said, 'I'll shield your movements from her view.'

'Good idea.'

We needed to get out of there fast.

As we approached her cage Lika went nuts, grabbing wildly at the blanket to try and see what Andre was up to. She managed to get hold of the blanket but Andre was ready and placed the dart on the inside of her left thigh. It was lights out for Lika in less than eight minutes. I had obtained the key to her cage on an earlier occasion and I unlocked the cage door. It was difficult to get inside but I managed eventually to pick up her light body and hand her to Andre.

'We're going to have to carry her and the kit out in one go,' I said. 'We need to get her on the truck and get the hell out of here before the crowd comes pouring in to check on their friend.'

'He should be round by now,' Andre said and walked quickly back to the caretaker. Jacques had done a good monitoring job and all looked fine – except that he wasn't yet conscious and his eyes were rolling around in their sockets.

'It must be a good movie,' I said with a weak attempt at humour.

'I believe you're right ... you stay here and I'll keep an eye on Lika.'

I put some water in the caretaker's eyes and settled down beside him. It was another thirty minutes before he showed the first signs of regaining consciousness.

As he opened his eyes, Jacques and I hurried off to join Andre.

'Okay, let's go! Hurry!'

Andre had wrapped Lika in the same blanket that I'd used. We grabbed opposite ends and made our way out of the store towards the truck parked thirty yards down the street. The crowd just looked on, evidently still satisfied with our earlier explanation. Soon they would probably want reassurance that their friend was in good health. I left Andre and Lucinda to take care of Lika while I went to deal with the lynch mob.

I grabbed the translator by the arm and led him to the caretaker. His head was bobbing around as though he was intoxicated, but he was definitely coming round.

'See, he is on a wild ride,' I said, wiping the sweat from my face. 'Tell him we are really, really sorry this happened and I'll make it up to him next time I'm in the neighbourhood. Here's fifty dollars.'

I didn't waste time waiting for a reply. I walked hurriedly back to the truck, jumped in the back and thumped the roof of the cab to indicate I was ready to go. The driver put his foot on the accelerator and we sped off to our final location which was less than thirty minutes' drive through the now deserted midnight streets.

Once again we'd had to handle a tricky situation. It seemed Murphy was throwing everything he could find at us. But we were so close now, just Xinga and Mimi to be collected. I was both physically and mentally exhausted but the thought of being close to achieving what we'd set out to do kept me focused. At the back of my mind I was still thinking about things for which I had no Plan B – for example, if the truck broke down, or if we were unable to immobilise the last two chimps. Realistically, I suppose, it wasn't possible to cover every detail when the plan kept changing.

When we arrived at the liqueur bottling factory we found that the owner, Mr Carmo, and a lot of his workers had stayed up to bid the chimps farewell. There was also another reason. After the last escape the cage door had been welded closed and would have to be cut open with an angle grinder to gain access. The idea of the chimps being held in a cage that couldn't be opened was sickening; then again, if they'd managed to escape they might have suffered the same fate as their dead sister.

Carmo had placed spotlights everywhere so that the whole area was well lit. I directed all the spotlights on to the cage, completely blinding Mimi and Xinga. This gave Andre the advantage of being able to get close enough to shoot accurately, and he would need to because there was an additional complication. The facilities did not allow us to separate the two chimps which meant both had to be darted at the same time. If we managed to dart only one chimp the whole exercise would have been pointless because we weren't able to access the cage unless both were anaesthetised. Murphy hadn't finished his work either. Twice Andre released the dart and twice the dart did not eject its contents. Each dart is pressurised prior to the drug contents being loaded and on rare occasions this fails to deliver the drugs instantly through the syringe before the chimp pulls the dart out.

Andre was getting frustrated and the chimps were getting agitated and I didn't blame them; they couldn't see who was attacking them and of course they couldn't understand why. It was third time lucky for Andre as far as Xinga was concerned. The dart hit home and pretty soon Xinga was snoozing away in the front of the cage. By this time Mimi was completely bewildered. She could see what had happened to her sister and intelligently positioned herself in a corner and held up a blanket in front of her, and she did this so well that the chance to dart her was thwarted. The drugs we were using did not give any guarantee of exactly how long a chimpanzee would be unconscious and the longer we struggled, the worse our chances became of completing the mission. Added to this was the worry of what effect the adrenalin levels of the chimps might have. They had both been so hyped up, creating concern that one or both might suddenly wake up, exposing all of us to the risk of injury.

After about twenty minutes of battling Andre finally got the shot, the dart flying straight and true and hitting Mimi in the upper thigh, the only part of her body that wasn't hidden under the blanket at the time. Now it was time for the grinders. As they dug into the welded arches around the door it was obvious that the welding had been done so well that there was no chance of the door ever again being functional. It was the point of no return and it was another big moment for me when the screeching of the grinders stopped and the door fell to the ground with a loud clank. The cage that had confined both these chimps had been destroyed. I climbed through the small opening armed only with a broomstick and slowly and softly prodded both animals to make sure they were asleep. Next came the blankets and then one at a time we moved them to the crates at the back of the truck. Zac was now fully awake and vocalised softly when he heard us. The two sleeping females were given their reversal drug and Lucinda kept an eye on them while Andre and I got ready to leave.

There was an all-round mood of jubilation as we slowly realised that all the chimps were now on the truck and the only trip left was the one to the airport. It was, of course, still a long way to South Africa but the most difficult part of the journey was over. It was 2am when we departed on the thirty-minute drive to the airport. If all went well, we would be exactly on time.

The driver got us to the airport in good time. There were no problems about checking in the chimps. Tom had followed us in his own vehicle for most of the evening and he made sure the security staff gave us every assistance as the crates were offloaded. Stickers and paperwork were attached to each crate. It was important to keep the chimps as stress-free as possible so that they would be able to sleep. They were all calm except for Mimi and Xinga who cried for each other constantly, taking turns in vocalising and answering. The two sisters were obviously devoted to each other. On a number of occasions Xinga stretched herself out to her full length, levering against the back of the crate as she pushed at the wooden door outside the metal cage. The door bulged a bit but it held, at least for the time being; there was no knowing if it would last for the whole flight. There was no real possibility of her escaping because the steel cage was immensely strong, but if the door came off she'd be able to reach out and grab at things, including people.

The crates would be placed on an aluminium pallet and secured to it with cargo nets which was an added dimension of security. But in my exhausted state my vivid imagination went to work: what would happen if a chimp escaped on the plane? Would we crash? Would the passengers go crazy? What would I do? I almost drove myself nuts before I managed to block all such thoughts out of my mind. These chimps were going to South Africa, come hell or high water!

At around 4am the loading crew prepared the crates and transported them to the aircraft. They were unloaded on to the tarmac where they were visible from the terminal. Tom kept an eye on them – more particularly on Xinga – while we checked in. Then for two hours I watched the crates from the building until eventually it was time for us to board. But I was uneasy. Something was telling me that I needed to make absolutely sure that the chimps were loaded on to the plane and so I left my seat and went out of the door and stood on the stairway. I had a clear view of the crates from there and would be able to watch them being loaded on to the plane through the rear cargo door.

The loading process involved a vehicle with a telescopic platform called a container loader which lifted pallets and unit load devices to the same level as the cargo door where it was pushed into the cargo bay of the aircraft. My spirits rose as the pallet containing the crates was jacked up to the level of the cargo door. There was no stopping us now! The container loader operator stopped and walked past the crates into the cargo bay. On his way back disaster struck: a hairy hand scrabbled wildly under the netting. This must have been a terrible shock to the operator as he leapt from the platform to the ground, a distance of about 12 feet.

I closed my eyes and covered my face with my hands. Surely we'd be kicked off the flight now, the chimps would never see freedom and if they weren't shot by the security officials the best they could look forward to was returning to their miserable cages.

'Give me a break!' I yelled at the heavens before running down the stairs to the operator.

Surprisingly, he was on his feet. I apologised profusely but I was lucky for once: the guy had a sense of humour and just smiled at me and said something in Portuguese before he returned to his loader. The flight stewardess, however, was humourless and sternly ushered me back on to the plane, waving her hands and muttering what sounded to me like swearwords. From the top of the stairs I saw the crates enter the aircraft and the operator looked at me and shook his head.

Yes, I know I'm bloody crazy, they're just monkeys, I thought as I boarded the plane.

There were a few surprises at the South African end of the journey which delayed us unnecessarily, but the chimps all made it to Chimp Eden. Today they are a thriving family enjoying the freedom they'd been denied for so long. This was a mission from hell, but it is also one of my proudest achievements.

SUDAN

Right up to the point of sitting at the airstrip with five chimpanzees screaming their heads off and a plane that wouldn't be landing to take us all home, this has been another mission cursed by Murphy. Years of rescuing chimps from multiple locations all over the world have provided me with enough experience to have counter-measures in place to deal with Murphy's unpredictability. Murphy has become an actual person to me, even though he is only supposed to be a law. Somewhere, somehow, there is a cosmic power at work and its aim is to test me to my limits.

Although I am a devout Christian, I have my own beliefs about talking to God. I believe that He has provided me with the wisdom and strength necessary to do my work. I don't believe things are going to unfold miraculously just because I have asked God for it to happen. I have to use my own abilities to determine my fate and if I mess up, then it is on my own head. I prefer to be in control of my own destiny.

Now, in this impossible situation in which I find myself, I finally accept that there is a limit to my own abilities. I have no back-up plan. The next flight available for us to leave Sudan with the chimps will be by the same company in eight months' time. Murphy has me in checkmate. I look at the people who are with me and am reminded of the time I had to tell Mr da Silva that his chimp wouldn't be leaving Luanda – a moment that is etched in my memory for ever.

Under the tree with the three crates Sue is still doing her best to calm the chimps. Cameraman Willem Ludwich and director Anton Trusdale are also sitting under the tree. Since I agreed to take part in the Animal Planet series 'Escape to Chimp Eden' the two of them have travelled with me on a few occasions. I like them, they are both good guys but they are under enormous pressure making the series and it is essential that they return to South Africa with a successful rescue on record. They have been with me here in Rumbek for over a month filming every day of the caretaking operations as well as some adventures in search of chimpanzees being sold in markets. Even though they are both aware of the risks involved in what I do for a living, they aren't going to take it well when I tell them that the mission is a failure. Annie Olivecrona is also trying to keep the chimps calm. She has been in Sudan for some time, looking after the chimps on behalf of the Jane Goodall Institute Kenya who are very much involved with conservation issues in the region.

Only the film crew, Annie and I are supposed to be leaving on the flight with the chimps, but it is especially important for Sue Knight that the mission succeeds. She was looking forward to a positive ending to her part of the story. She will take the news worst of all.

I muster up the guts to walk over to the group. They can sense something is wrong and they all look up as I approach.

'The plane can't land,' I say. 'It seems the tower in El Obeid has threatened trouble if they attempt to land here.'

'What the hell? Why?' Sue demands.

'Something about the clearance being revoked. Fact is, there is nothing we can do about it.'

Anton gets up from under the tree. 'What do we do now?' he asks.

'Worst case scenario is the chimps go back to the house and we get the next plane out of here. I'm tapped out completely ... the minister's little party cleaned me out so I can't afford another charter.'

Annie had organised the necessary permits with the deputy head of the wildlife conservation administration a few weeks earlier, but in a bizarre twist of events the minister of environmental affairs for Southern Sudan declared that he would be giving the chimps a personal send-off during a lavish banquet and he travelled from Juma to Rumbek with his entourage for the occasion. Covering the cost would be my honour. Well, in a place like this if you want the job done you've got to roll with the punches and keep smiling.

The minister had kept his word and his 'farewell banquet' and the cost of his airplane ticket meant that I was out of pocket. But we didn't have too much choice. Everything else was paid for – Safair had been paid five thousand dollars to divert and land at the Rumbek airfield, then we'd have an overnight stop in Uganda and continue on to South Africa the next morning. Safair is a privately owned airline that provides the

UN Food Programme, amongst others, with C-130 aircraft. Once a year the aircraft returns to its base in Entebbe in Uganda and in this instance we'd be flying back to South Africa with the same Safair plane with the chimps rather than transferring them to a commercial flight.

'So we use the tickets we were issued as a back-up measure?' Anton asks.

I nod. As a back-up plan, in case things went wrong, we have tickets for a small plane that flies a commercial route from Nairobi in Kenya to Rumbek. But this isn't an option for the chimps because the plane is too small.

I lean against one of the crates and a small finger emerges and plucks at my trousers. I bend down and look through the breathing hole. It's Nina. Not exactly the cutest chimp in the group, she is the oldest and is sometimes aggressive so I thought it best she complete the journey in a crate of her own.

They are a lively bunch of chimpanzees. Nina, the oldest and the only female, is four; Thomas, the oldest male, is a similar age, and Zee, Dinka and Charlie are all about one and a half years old. The three youngsters are an appealing bunch and it will break my heart not to get them to freedom – but what am I to do? Logistics and budgetary constraints will only make it possible for us to return for another attempt when the next flight is available, which could be anywhere from six to twelve months.

With no commercial flights available in Southern Sudan that connect to an international airport, our options are confined to depending on Safair for their routine maintenance flights. There is a good chance that I will never see any of these chimps again if I have to abandon them now.

236

'Can you think of any other options?' I ask despairingly. 'I sure as hell can't.'

'What about the other charter company Jan told you about?' Sue jogs my memory.

'Not an option. Originally, they wanted twenty-five thousand dollars to fly us to South Africa.'

There were quite a few charter companies operating in and around the central belt of Africa; if you could find an airfield you could probably find a charter outfit. The problem was that their charges were enormous and completely unaffordable as far as we were concerned.

'Is there no way the UN will help us out?' Sue asks.

'No,' I reply. 'My knees are already bleeding as a result of all the begging I've done with them. They have regulations against transporting animals, even rescue efforts.'

The UN had planes landing at Rumbek two to three times a day, not to mention the MI-8 helicopters that were a dime a dozen. Their job was to 'observe' and offer humanitarian assistance. To a simple man like me it is obvious: if you have space in the plane after helping people, why not help an animal? Most of the aircraft located at Rumbek took off without cargo and flew to destinations that were useful in chimp rescue work. But our cause was not deemed sufficiently important, especially in a region on the verge of war. The southern Sudanese people were tired of being controlled by the North Sudan government in Khartoum. They felt that they had been cheated out of the revenue of oil operations in the south and were willing to fight to the death to get control of what was rightfully theirs. It wasn't an unusual African scenario.

Unfortunately, during times of unrest the environment and wildlife get no consideration at all, being regarded merely as 'casualties' of war. The priorities are providing food and other vital supplies for both troops and civilians, not whether or not an entire animal species is wiped out. People will always receive preferential treatment and I have never understood why this should be so. After all, is it really worth being alive if the earth has been reduced to ash? Our irresponsible attitude towards our environment will have only one outcome.

I look at my watch nervously. Time for making a plan is running out. The Safair plane is no longer an option; it had left El Obeid earlier that morning and had already overflown us. I walk towards the Land Cruiser where our suitcases and film equipment are packed. I am feeling both desperate and defeated. I open the door of the vehicle and dig through the contents of my bag looking for any information that will give me an idea for a solution. I am usually quick on my feet, but not now.

I run different ideas through my head. Drive the chimps out in the Land Cruiser with a makeshift trailer attached to it? No, that will take at least seven days on account of the terrible roads. Fly them to Khartoum and from there to Uganda to catch our Safair flight? No, not enough time and moreover we don't have visas for the north.

Think, dammit, think!

I sigh heavily and rest my head on the back seat. I need your help on this one, God. I am not asking for a miracle; I am only asking you for the wisdom to solve the problem, and the rest I will do myself.

And then, like a bolt of lightning, it strikes me. Safair has been paid five thousand dollars to pick us up in Rumbek. Can I get them to pay another charter company to come and get us and fly us to Entebbe in time to catch the Safair plane before it takes off for South Africa?

I run back to Sue. 'Can you find the number for the charter company in Nanyuki? Can you phone them quickly and ask them if we can take them up on the offer to fly us, but only from here to Entebbe? Tell them Safair will pay them five thousand dollars as soon as they land there.'

'Okay.'

She makes the call and I can tell from the tone of the conversation that things are going our way. Sue's contact is a good friend who believes in the work we are doing.

'They say they're pulling the seats out of a plane that is about to take off,' Sue tells me. 'They will be here in a few hours.'

The plane they will send is a single engine Cessna that will usually seat up to ten people. They are removing the seats to make space for the crates.

'YES!'

Everyone bursts into excited laughter when they hear this. Unfortunately, with the soldiers sitting only a few yards away, there is no opportunity for Willem to capture this moment on film.

I call Darian at the Safair headquarters in South Africa. 'I have a plan,' I tell him. 'If you can help out we can still make this work.'

I tell him what my plan is, explaining that his role is to ensure the cash is available in Entebbe for the charter company, as well as helping us to load the chimps on to their C-130 cargo plane. This could be a tricky situation because we don't have transit permits. We wouldn't have needed them if we'd only be stopping to refuel – which was the original plan – but now we will be changing planes. One can never predict what will happen if the authorities find fault with your paperwork – jail time or a fine perhaps, but the chimps could face confiscation.

But we have a plan now and I am going to do whatever it takes to see it through.

The chartered Cessna arrives about four hours later and everyone pitches in to help carry the crates the one hundred or so yards past the soldiers to the aircraft. Miraculously, they let us pass. Our manifests and shipping documents were issued before we left South Africa and all we needed from the Sudanese Customs officials was their stamp of approval. Our strategy of using the 'back door' to get the chimps on the plane will work as long as Sue's contact comes through for us by getting the shipping documents stamped, and he does. After less than thirty minutes on the ground, including refuelling, we are in the air en route to Entebbe.

My heart skips a beat as the wheels lift off the ground. We are finally on our way. All I can do is hope that the plan works because there are still so many factors outside my control. It is a five-hour flight from Rumbek to Entebbe, but Murphy is not going to make it easy. The weather starts breaking up about two hours into the flight. Gigantic cumulonimbus cloud formations (or Charlie Bravos, as pilots call them) begin rising thousands of feet up into the air, completely dwarfing our small aircraft.

I know that if the pilot cannot find a way through the bad weather he will have to change course and I constantly pester him with this question. At 12 000 feet we have a spectacular view of the forests beneath us and I can't help but wonder how many of our chimp cousins are still living there. According to statistics, there is something in the region of 100 000 chimps remaining in the wild, but I'm not so sure.

The flight takes two hours longer than expected because of all the course corrections the pilot has to make, but he lands us on the apron at Entebbe safe and sound. This is the moment I have been worrying about throughout the flight. Annie, the film crew and I get out along with the pilots making sure all the doors are closed so that chimp vocalisations do not attract unwanted attention. We walk to the terminal building where we find a Customs official in a glass cubicle. The pilots hand over their paperwork and say that they have to taxi to the UN section of the airfield, as the passengers and cargo are intended for them.

'Anything to declare?' – the words I have been dreading. I am sure we should say something about the chimps but, as one, we reply 'Nothing!' The Customs official looks up at us for a moment, hands back our passports and motions with his hand that we should move on.

'Just keep calm,' I tell myself, fighting the urge to yell with excitement.

The chimps seem to have sensed my excitement as some of them are shouting incredibly loudly. Fortunately there is no one on the tarmac to hear them.

We board the plane again and taxi to the UN compound where a C-130 is waiting for us, door open and ready. I am so overjoyed to see them that I give the first crew member I see a big hug – which I guess is pretty weird. The chimps are transferred to the bigger aircraft and with all the formalities wrapped up I can now breathe a sigh of relief.

My entire family is waiting at the airport in Johannesburg, including my wife who is in the last months of pregnancy. Twenty-four hours later we reach Chimp Eden without a hitch.

◇

The three weeks in Sudan have been a wild experience during which I have travelled to isolated and dangerous areas. There were countless setbacks and problems, but I was experienced now in sorting out the inevitable difficulties a rescue mission encounters and although Murphy was along with me, conjuring up every obstacle imaginable, I managed to overcome them all. They included the Safair flight being postponed twice, a sandstorm putting the airfield out of commission, permit and blood sampling issues and then – just to crown everything, the minister deciding to throw a party at our expense.

There have been many times during the years of rescue missions and the rehabilitation of chimpanzees when I feel I cannot continue to deal with the stress that comes with my work but, always, it is the animals that drive me back. I don't think the enslavement of primates will ever be eradicated but I like to think that people like my family and dedicated individuals like Phillip, Doug, Sue, Monique* and Alissa, and the many others who are part of the Pan African Sanctuary Alliance and the Jane Goodall Institute are buying time for the great ape families in the wild and giving a new lease on life to those whose freedom was denied them.

---

* Not their real names.

AFTERWORD

Shortly after we left Lebanon the first Israeli bombs were dropped on Beirut making an already difficult situation even worse for the BETA team. This dedicated group that worked hard to liberate the captive chimpanzees split into two different organisations – BETA remained as one and the second became known as Animals Lebanon. Both these bodies work tirelessly to rescue orphaned animals and they do so without government funding. Monique and Alissa head up the respective organisations and I'm proud to have worked alongside them.

After we left Lebanon the chimps were returned to their cages, with the exception of one. We were correct in our suspicion that the so-called 'death' of the chimps was merely a ploy to manipulate weak laws. To this day there has been no further effort at confiscation. The two organisations have, however, been successful in rescuing and relocating several baboons and are working on the relocation of one chimpanzee to Brazil. Although I had my differences with Mark,* his commitment was never in doubt and he now works alongside Alissa in running Animals Lebanon.

When I reflect on the time I have spent with Cozy, Joao, Zeena and Sally, I know that these were some of the best moments in my life. Cozy is now the third ranking male in his group and Joao has relinquished his alpha status to Zac. Zac's progress was exceptional, especially considering that he was in the poorest condition of any animal we have rescued.

The birth of our daughter Haley was the start of a whole new adventure for Natasha and me. The responsibilities that came with parenthood brought more changes to my life. I decided to take fewer chances with rehabilitation efforts and I limit the time I spend in the enclosures. More people have since joined our team and are doing well. I'd like to think that JGI South Africa and the team will continue with their dedicated and inspiring work regardless of whether or not I am involved. This, and the longevity of the sanctuary, is my greatest wish.

I hope that the sanctuary will be a lasting legacy for my family who gave everything they had to ensure that it would succeed. It was built with their blood, sweat and tears and they have my endless gratitude. Jane Goodall has been my inspiration and her continued support has motivated all of us. Her dedication and her work have inspired millions and her active campaigning has, without doubt, been significant in ensuring the survival of the chimpanzee. Edwin Jay, chairman of JGI South Africa, and Sue Slotar, former director of JGI South Africa, have

---

* Not his real names.

played a monumental role in getting the sanctuary to where it is today and I thank them most sincerely.

At the time of going to press the sanctuary is home to thirty-three chimpanzees . . . and growing.

I have never abused my responsibility for chimp rehabilitation for exploitative reasons, and any member of my family who has been involved had a vital role to play. During the filming of the Animal Planet series 'Escape to Chimp Eden', I did my best to bring the plight of orphaned and abused chimpanzees to public notice. With viewers of the series numbering in the hundreds of millions I hope I have been successful in achieving this.

After the screening of the series there were many requests for interviews, almost all of which wanted me to appear with a live chimpanzee. They were never done. My refusal to do so was because of my belief that every single wild animal has the right to an existence free of human interference and exploitation. The chimpanzees that will live out their lives at the sanctuary may not be in their natural environment but what we offer them is the best we can do and is surely vastly better than the conditions we rescued them from. Our efforts may seem futile to many a critic but we believe that every individual matters and the efforts to save them, combined with media exposure, can change the world.

As I reflect on the last few years of my life, fighting as hard as I can to rescue just a few chimpanzees, I realise that it is not enough to save them from extinction. It doesn't even come close. But I am content to know that I have made a difference. The chimps I have rescued are more than just a cause I believe in, they are my friends, and I'd do it all over again in a heartbeat.